Violence:
It's Causes and Cure

Violence:
It's Causes and Cure

Violence: Ending or Don't Hold Your Breath?

Jack Eden

Writers Club Press
San Jose New York Lincoln Shanghai

Jack and Joanne whose help was essential to

the completion of the work.

Contents

Introduction

There are many people that would begin to read a paper such as this one on violence and as soon as I touch on their pet philosophy they would stop reading. It seems that many people have such a mind set about certain things or certain philosophies that nothing short of dynamite is going to budge their minds off high center. They don't even realize that they are spinning their wheels.

I've been amazed in the last few years at how so many people can see one color when the color has been proven to be some other color. If you were looking at something red, would it not seem foolish to call it green? They just won't see the true color because they don't want to do so. It's sort of like sticking your head in the sand-but that's for ostriches isn't it? Let's look at the problem another way. If you had a real bad wound, in order to find out how bad it was and what was necessary to get it healed, you would have to probe the wound. Now that probing might not be very pleasant and some people would not want it done perhaps because they would be afraid of what they would find in the wound. But you would not want the doctor to sew up the wound and sew up a big clod of dirt inside it would you? Well maybe some people would.

I had the interesting experience of running for a public office some years back and as I went door to door and talked with the people I realized just how little reasoning and presentation of facts meant to a lot of people. Not all voters, but many. (Some voters were very careful and very well informed.) Many were totally blind to anything but what they had done all their lives, issues made no difference, only customs and habits. Only

God could make any changes in some peoples thinking and He won't do it unless He is allowed to do so.

Let's hope anyway that you read to the end and see what the answers might be, and then if you think it is possible to reach the goal of a less violent, more gentle, more loving society in which we live. In Chapter One let's take a look at some of the problems of today and some future problems.

Chapter One

The Problem and Future Problems

The mental processes of wanting to write began shortly after I listened to a very closed minded big shot that gave his ideas on how to stop the violence in America. As he talked my blood pressure rose point by point. It was one of those talks that gave no room to ask a question, as the guy was much too important to have his train of thoughts interrupted. So I wrote down a number of questions as he talked, figuring there would be the usual question and answer session after the lecture. But no! The big shot took off from the meeting before anyone could ask him a single question about his philosophy. Since I had made a list of questions and thoughts about his talk, I was disappointed to say the least. As a result I wrote an article that was published in the April 1994 issue of *Law and Order Magazine*. The article was more or less a rebuttal to the big shot's talk. I doubt that he ever read the article since he probably knew all the answers to stopping violence, he probably would not be reading a law enforcement magazine with educational material in it.

Since that publication I've gotten positive feedback from across the United States. Because of that feedback and the support that was given to me locally, I decided to really get with the program and really go into detail about crime and violence, their causes and possible cures, and probably make a lot of people mad at me in the process. I'm sure that some of the guilty people will rationalize their actions and say, "He's not talking about me.", just as I'm sure that some of the totally innocent people, nice people, will say, "He's talking about me." If the guilty and the innocent would really think clearly for a few moments, without letting personal prejudices enter in, but that might be too hard for some to do.

I realize the thinking of a lot of people in the United States is not the same as out here in the Great Plains. I realize too, that many of the liberal, bleeding heart ideas of the left wing thinkers has crept into the minds of some even out here. While teaching and while serving in law enforcement I had contact with many people, such as teachers, preachers, parents, teenagers, etc., and I noticed the liberal ideas seemed to be cropping up more and more often.

As I write it occurs to me that not only will this thesis make everybody angry, but it might seem that there are no answers. It may look like there is no way out of the mess that we're in at the present. That isn't quite so, since there is a way to correct the problems we face today. There is a way to stop the violence and even more importantly keep it from getting worse as other problems arise. There is a way out, as you will see in Chapter Eleven. (Or at least you will be exposed to the answer.) But the question will still be, will mankind take that way, or will he drift ever deeper into the quicksand of chaos and violence?

In the last few years there have been a number of movies or TV shows that depict a world after some catastrophe. A germ war, or a nuclear war, or some natural disaster that nearly annihilates mankind. (And womankind.) A world left devastated, dirty, without modern conveniences, such as electricity, fuel, water, transportation, etc. A world where food and other resources are more valuable than gold. A world where the weak are terrorized and enslaved by the strongest. A world ruled by the most violent types of humanity. A world where life is very cheap and to kill for little or no reason at all seem to be the norm. (I'm talking about some movies, not some of our present day big cities.) Now that first movie or two seemed pretty ridiculous. They had to be made by someone whose imagination was just running wild, or maybe they were intoxicated when they wrote the script. But as you watch not the movies, but the newscasts today, and see the violence, the chaos, the hunger, that is going on in this world right now, it would not take too many catastrophes to actually bring on what you see in some of those far out movies. At the present time the possibilities for military action, even war, in a number of places on this planet are just pretty good. Some of these areas you would not think of as hot spots on the globe. Some of these governments have biological weapons, nuclear weapons, or chemical weapons. Since terrorist activities are the cheapest means of fighting a war, who is to say that one of those renegade little governments, or a big one, isn't going to use some of those weapons of mass destruction? Even though the United States is supposed to be the most powerful nation in the world, (which I wonder about as our armed forces get smaller and smaller and more dependent on electronic gadgetry that can get fouled up with who knows what.) With some of the chemical and biological weapons it would not be too difficult to produce devastation such as you would find in one of those movies. Then the violence you would see would chill you to the bone. But don't give up. Remember there is a way out if mankind is willing to pay the price. The article I wrote for *Law and Order* was of what it would take to stop the violence that seems to be escalating all over the world, and especially here at home in the United States. Originally I took up pen as protest against a philosophy that irritated me deeply. (I call it a philosophy because I believe the whole plan behind gun control is a philosophy that could lead to disaster.) Uh Oh. Now I've slipped and told you what irritated me in the first place. You'll probably think right wing kook and burn the book. But gun control is just the tip of the iceberg.

I could not understand why so many of the left-wingers could feel that the answer to so many of the world's problems, especially violence in the United States, could be gun control. (It seemed that if someone got stabbed to death, there would be a bill introduced someplace in congress to outlaw guns. Or if someone got bashed in the head with a ball bat, there was the howl and cry, outlaw guns.) At the time it seemed very stupid to think that the criminal would give up his gun, especially when the population as a whole was unarmed and ripe for the picking.

In trying to understand this philosophy that says that gun control will stop crime and violence and usher in the age of Utopia, I had to look at a much broader spectrum than crime, violence, and gun control. What came to mind was a picture that wasn't very pretty at all. Some of the things that developed indicated that we haven't seen violence at all yet, but to see the whole picture we'll have to delve into several areas that have much to do with violence, yet may seem unrelated.

I remember a class entitled Human Ecology taken in the summer of 1972 at what is now Emporia University, at Emporia, Kansas. I was taking some post graduate work and the class sounded like it would provide some good material for my Biology classes. We studied many facets of ecology that summer. We studied human population and its explosive growth on a worldwide scope. We studied food, its production, its shortages, and future demands. Pollution of all kinds was a big thing then, the different kinds, air, water, soil were studied. Waste materials, such as garbage, plastic, paper, rubber, metal, nuclear, and even human and animal wastes, were considered, especially how to get rid of them. Raw materials, their use, depletion, and total exhaustion were all considered. We pretty well covered the whole spectrum of life on planet earth. The conclusions the class reached were the same as the conclusions that had been reached in a study done a few years prior to our study when all the data had been fed into computers. At that time the computers concluded that if mankind continued in the way it was going, there would be a total collapse of all systems here on earth by the year two thousand. We reached the same conclusions. But there was an alternative.

The alternative was that mankind, on a world wide basis, not just in the United States, had to completely change its selfish ways and begin to consider the effects his or her lifestyle had on the rest of the world. (We in the United States have a very difficult time considering the rest of the world in problems like this because we are here and the rest of the world is someplace else, almost like it's on another planet. The rest of the world is getting closer by the day as faster means of travel and communication seem to shrink the globe. As we watch the starvation, the violence, the atrocities, in other countries in the news, it is all brought much closer home to us. Television for the past few years has been bringing the problems of the world into our living rooms but the Internet through computers is going to bring it all right into our laps.)

There was a time limit set for this change of heart that the world was supposed to have. At the time the members of my class couldn't see how mankind could change even with more time than the computers gave. Sure enough, the years went by, the time limit came and went and mankind not only had no change of heart, but he has grown more self-centered as the years have gone by.

Now the year two thousand has wound down. You say, "I see no evidence that there is about to be a collapse of all the world systems." You see no changes? You never had it so good? You see no signs of the times? Let's for a moment consider some of the areas that we studied over twenty years ago in the Ecology class.

Take population for example. You say the United States has really cut down on the population growth rate? Yes, it has cut down on the rate of growth statistically. It is within what you might call acceptable limits to keep things stable, at least on paper it is. Consider the following four points however.

Of course when the population of a nation gets so great that that nation can't support it, many try to get to some place where they can survive. That's called immigration. (After all, if you can get into the United States you can get a job, even a low paying job is more than they could make elsewhere. Then if you can get on welfare, get food stamps, get free medical help, free schooling, etc., it's worth a try anyway. Nothing to lose and everything to gain.)

Note the thousands of Mexican immigrants, mostly illegal, coming into the Untied States. (I guess the term Mexican is a no no, we're supposed to call them Hispanic, which doesn't change a thing, since most Hispanics come from Mexico.)

Note the shiploads of Haitians, Cubans, and the Chinese trying to enter the United States. The ship load of Chinese that tried to get into the

United States and would have succeeded had it not gotten caught when it ran aground off the east coast. That story was on the news for weeks.

But for all that there are untold thousands of illegal immigrants that do succeed in getting in and swelling the population of the United States and these don't make the news at all.

Now we do have an immigration service that's supposed to take care of all that illegal immigration. Bull! While in law enforcement we caught a number of illegal immigrants. Most of them were of Hispanic origin coming through town on the northbound train. For a while we would stop the train just outside of town and take the individual or individuals into custody. None ever had any form of Ids, money, or rudiments of the English language. We would get the high school Spanish teacher to come down and try to get basic information from them. That didn't get much usually. Now we always notified the immigration service of what we had and the answer was always the same. If what we had in custody was a busload of illegals, they would send someone down to take care of the problem. If what we had was one or two individuals, they didn't have the manpower to be bothered. Since it was always one or two at the most, at any one time, we always wound up feeding them a meal and turning them loose to either find their fortune farther north, or to be picked up again by some other law enforcement agency on up the line. Some of those that went on north had tattoos that indicated they had or had had gang connections. (I remember one that the Spanish teacher talked to, after we had no luck with him at all. She said, "I followed his conversation until he got to telling about the cockroaches in his head. He lost me there." We had to let him go, but we all felt he did have cockroaches in his head.)

So we are picking up a lot of population from immigration. Now if our population is fairly stable, what is happening to keep it that way? Point number three might be that many couples are holding off having children until later in life, or not having any children at all. This would have a neutralizing effect on our population.

Another aspect of our population, point four, is that a lot of our growth is cut down by abortion. Simply by murdering unborn children the growth rate drops. (As does the moral values of our people.) I guess I shouldn't use the term murder for abortion, after all I wouldn't want to make fifteen or twenty million women angry with me because of semantics. Substitute killing babies for murder. Maybe it will sound smoother, more civilized, gentler.

I've read that there have been some twenty million abortions performed in the last twenty or so years. If those twenty million babies had lived, some of them would be producing children by now. Yes, abortion does have an effect on population. (And we are wondering where the young workers are going to come from that will pay for Medicare and social security in a few generations? Many of them got buried before they were born.)

Another thought here is the increasing age of the population after we eliminate, spelled abort, the very young. The illegals that are coming in are not very young either. I wonder if anyone has stopped to consider that if you kill off all the young, the unborn, the growth rate might drop to zero. We would become extinct. Don't worry about becoming extinct though, we'll never last that long anyway. But at the rate we are going we could become a nation of non-producing old codgers. Who would do the producing then? Who would pay for taking care of all us seventy, eighty, or ninety-year olds? Do you suppose the illegal immigrants would take on that task? I think not. More on who will take care of you when you reach that ripe old age later.

A side issue here is if the nation becomes a nation of old folks and one of those hungry third world nations with a high birth rate and millions of young men decides that we can't cut the mustard anymore, what will stop them from coming over and taking over. (Now don't tell me our high tech electronic gadgetry will stop them. I've seen too many computers go on the blink to trust my life to a computer controlled defense mechanism.)

Speaking of abortion, it's interesting to consider how abortion has expanded its boarders. It no longer is a procedure whereby a two or three month old baby embryo is killed, but it can go right up to the full nine months when the baby is turned in such a way as to be delivered feet first, then when the baby is delivered all but the head, an instrument is inserted into the base of the skull, killing it. (A little legal point there. It wouldn't do to allow the baby to be born all the way, then kill it. That would be not only illegal, but immoral.) This partial birth procedure is supposed to be to protect the mother. For the baby to be completely born is supposed somehow to endanger the mother, so it's partially born, then killed. I always thought to have a baby born feet first was rather hard on the mother, but then, what do I know? It just seems it would be easier on the mother to have a normal childbirth than to turn the baby in uteri so that it would pass down the birth canal feet first, but again, what do I know?

I've heard rumors that the baby isn't wasted after being killed, its' organs can be used for transplants or experiments. Does that remind you of the movie, "Coma"? I'm sure that some of the doctors doing the killing would charge the same for a liver transplant from a killed baby as they would for any other transplant. But those rumors were probably started by some fanatical individual in a panic to save a few lives. Lately a number of states have passed laws outlawing partial birth abortions. Usually however there is a qualifier in the law that says, 'unless the mothers health is in danger'. Bull. If the mother's health is endangered by the baby it sure isn't going to be made any better by having the baby turned and born feet first. It's just a loophole that will be used every time they want to do a late abortion.

At the other end of life it's interesting to consider what might happen to all those old folks. Those old folks that a financially strapped world wouldn't be able to support. Especially if food and energy is at a premium. It might be that programs such as Medicare would have to be eliminated for financial reasons, then with the extremely high costs of medical care the way it's going today, the old folks won't be able to afford medical care. Some may just die quickly for lack of medical care, but others that get sick and in pain might find kind hearted and caring people like Dr. Kavorkin, alias Dr. Death, ready and willing to prescribe a painless death pill. It seems there isn't any way to stop people like Dr. Kavorkin, and if he gets away with it, I'm sure that some of the abortionists would not turn down the chance to pick up a little extra pocket change by helping the old folks out of this life. After all, there isn't much difference in killing a baby and killing an old person. You think such stuff could never happen in our Christian nation? It is already happening and we haven't even gotten to the hard times yet. When the real hard times come, those old folks may not have to call for a Dr. Death. A government such as some people would like to see in power might decide when to do the calling for Dr. Death.

Enough of that depressing type stuff. Let's talk about something more pleasant. Food. It is a little hard for people in the United States to think about a shortage of food. I know there are thousands of people in the United States that go to bed hungry, if they have a bed to go to. There are thousands of poverty level people that are malnourished. But the average American is more likely to have a problem of eating too much than not having enough to eat. This is not the picture you see in the rest of the world. Those pictures you see on television where they show a starving child and want you to send them money, those are real pictures of real children, and they are starving for real. So, you say, why don't they raise more food and feed themselves? In different countries there are different answers to that question. It may be years of drought. It may be not enough till-able land. It may be that those in power, that have plenty of food, don't want those not in power to live. (Sometimes called ethnic cleansing.) Whatever the answer, the result is the same, hundreds of thousands starving to death.

I recall in the 1960's a farmer saying the United States could produce enough food to feed the world. His theory was that when the supply of food got short, we would just put a little more fertilizer on the crops and get a bigger yield. It sounded like fertilizer at the time, but not being a farmer, I didn't argue. When the oil embargo took place in the early seventies, and the price of oil went way up, and the fertilizer, which needs oil for its production, got scarce, and the price of it went out of sight, that should have been an indication of what would happen when our oil reserves are depleted. Where will the fertilizer come from, or the fuel to run those monster tractors? Our supply of oil is finite. There will be a day when the well runs dry. In this geographic area alone I know of hundreds of oil wells that are no longer producing oil. They've been pumped dry and the only use they're put to now is when the con artists try to talk someone with a little money into sinking that money into a get rich quick oil company. (The con artists gets rich quick. The investor gets a tax write off.)

O.K. So you're sure that your oil well is not going to go dry in your lifetime. Let's talk about something that effects our production of food more than any kind of fertilizer or cultivation. It's water. No matter how much fertilizer you have, if you don't have water the crops won't grow. What happens to our food supply then, when the rains don't come? It has happened before. It probably was before some of you were born. (I can barely remember parts of it.) It's interesting to think back to the 1930's when there was a terrific drought and the dust bowl was produced in the central part of the United States. That so called 'dust bowl' covered some 36,000,000 acres of ground. There were no crops produced in large parts of Texas, Oklahoma, and Kansas. The land became a desert. There have been several movies made trying to show the hard times when the farmers of those areas couldn't make a living and had to give up and move out. The movies really couldn't show the dry heat, wind, and dust. Always dust in the air. They couldn't show how the dust storms picked up the topsoil from one place and blew it into the next county or the next state. At that time the United States wasn't doing a very good job of feeding its own, let alone the rest of the world.

When the rains finally did come it took years for much of the land to be returned to productivity and some never was put back into production. I can remember as a boy down in Oklahoma hunting quail in fields that you could see traces of plow furrows in, but the land was too shot to even grow pasture. Clumps of brush here and there did make for good quail hunting though.

To help counteract any future dry spells the government began a huge conservation effort. They planted mile after hundreds of miles of windbreaks. These windbreaks were fencerows planted with rows of tall trees, then rows of medium height trees, and rows of short trees. This was so that any topsoil that was left would not be blown away if there were another drought. The windbreaks did a pretty good job, plus they provided a wonderful place for wildlife to propagate.

However, memory is short and money is powerful stimulant. Those windbreaks took up a lot of land. Think of a huge row of trees maybe fifty feed wide and running for miles. It meant a lot of acres were in those windbreaks. So now if you drive through the western parts of these states, the areas where the dust bowl really took place, you will find very few wind breaks. They are almost enough of an oddity to have historical markers placed by them to explain what they are and why they are there. Nearly all of the wind breaks have been bulldozed out in mans' reaching for a few more acres to plant to make a few more dollars as fast as he can. In many areas you will see huge fields with the crops coming right out to the edge of the highway. Not a thing in sight to slow the wind down. But we haven't had a huge drought in a long time. Man seems to be a little slow to learn and fast to forget.

You say a drought is no problem now because we use irrigation? (You sure say a lot of things.) We pump the water from way down deep and squirt it out onto those lush green fields of grain and other vegetables. Yes. And have you heard that the water table way down there below the earth's surface is dropping, dropping, dropping? Not much is said about it since you can't see the water table level. Some people don't even know there is such a thing, but it's there and it is important. You can't tell how much water is down there, but the farmers know it's harder to pump it out each year. Each year they have to go lower with their pumps to reach the water.

But deeper wells and bigger pumps will keep that green stuff (money) growing. At least for now.

The scientists have figured out that water pumped out of artesian wells for cropland take some six hundred years to percolate through the aqueduct from the Rocky Mountains to Kansas. The irrigators are taking the water out much faster than it's percolating in from the mountains. What happens when those pumps go slurp, slurp, and no water comes out? Year by year the level of the water hundreds of feed down below the surface gets farther down. It gets harder to get enough water to the surface to irrigate those crops. There's coming a time, at the rate we're going, when there will not be enough water to pump out, then what? With not enough rain to raise the crops they have been raising, and nothing to slow the wind down, when the soil dries out it may get mighty dusty. There wouldn't really have to be a drought to get a new dust bowl started, just a lack of water to irrigate. The crops that are raised on these lands are really necessary for our food, and for supplying food for other parts of the world.

In the 1960's my family and I visited a man made lake called Cedar Bluff out in western Kansas. We camped on a little bluff overlooking one arm of the lake. My sons ran through the water along the sandy shore below the bluff and had a great time. It was a beautiful spot. Twenty years later I visited that same lake and didn't recognize it, even though we camped on the same bluff. The arm of the lake was gone. In its place was a dense thicket of trees, shrubs, and weeds, No water. (We heard lots of pheasants crowing the next morning in the brush that had been part of a lake.) The main body of the lake, which had naturally been right up against the dam, was some distance away from the dam. You could drive over sandy trails through thick brush on what had been the lake bottom out to the water. The boat launching pads were not even near the water.

What had happened? According to the manager of the park, crop irrigation was using water faster than it was coming into the lake. Too much water was being used up stream plus water was filtering down toward the water table from the lake itself. Then too there hadn't been enough rain.

Result? The lake was dying. I haven't been out there for over ten years now, but I've read that abundant rainfall the past few years has brought the lake level back up, but I haven't read anything about any slow down in irrigation.

And what about drinking water? There are large cities that are desperately looking for new sources of water. Some are already piping water from streams or lakes a great distance from the city. Those cities or areas guard their water supply against water snitchers with a vengeance. This need for fresh drinking water is going to become a much larger problem in the years to come.

It is said that history often repeats itself. All that would be needed to produce a real food shortage, a real disaster, is a drought lasting two or three years. With the winds given free reign by the elimination of windbreaks, we could have a dust bowl that would make the 30's seem like a whirlwind in a sandbox. Then from where would your bread come? And who would feed the world then?

Now when food begins to get short there are going to be those that will try to fill their larder no matter what it takes to get the job done. When that happens, violence such as you would not believe is going to escalate. Can't happen? We are too civilized? Are we really? Or are we just leading sheltered lives? In Africa where drought and civil wars have cause terrible food shortages there are groups of people, (guess they call them tribes) that try to wipe out entire tribes or other groups that are of a different nature. This is not happening a hundred years ago but in the last ten years. In Europe there are ethnic groups trying to wipe out other ethnic groups. They call it ethnic cleansing. You thought that type of stuff passed away with Adolph Hitler? Nay, no, nay. These people, all of them, are supposed to be civilized too. They may dress differently than we and talk differently, but they are supposed to be civilized. But you put overpopulation, food shortages, and old hates all in the same basket and you have a formula for violence. With the violent crime rate we have in the United States already, I'd say we have enough violent people to produce a great deal of violence when it gets rougher. I know that you are being told that violence is slowing down.

You've been told that the rate of violent crimes has dropped dramatically. (It has in some areas where the people have been given the right to carry a concealed weapon. After all what self-respecting robber is going to try to rob someone that can shoot back?) But if you read the newspapers and watch the news, you'll hear of robbery, murder, rape, and other forms of violent crime. All three were in tonight's paper, pertaining to incidents that happened in this area. This area has relatively few people compared to the metropolitan areas where most crime seems to occur. This area is classed as a low crime rate area.

Enough on food. Let us consider pollution. Pollution by our waste materials. Wastes that are produced by our homes such as garbage, trash, and sewage. Wastes that are produced by our manufacturing plants, by our cars, by our nuclear power plants, on and on.

Do you remember the news stories of the barge load of garbage that was towed up and down the East Coast while they tried to find a place to dump? (No pun intended.) No one wanted a barge load of garbage. Everyone had enough of their own garbage to get rid of without taking on someone else's. Or how about the trainload of garbage that set in an eastern rail center while they tried to figure out who would accept the stuff. There were pictures of the stuff dripping yuck from the cars as it set there in the rail yard. Too bad the television couldn't bring the smells to their viewers as well as the sights. Those were just two highly advertised incidents. Not very big stuff at all really, compared to the waste material that's produced in one day in a big city.

The really big pollution problems you can't see. It's the sewage polluting our streams, lakes, and even our oceans that is the big stuff. Nearly every state has either streams or lakes that are on a list of bodies of water you can't eat fish from, drink water from, or even swim in. The water in many bodies of water you can use for drinking only after it has undergone extensive and expensive treatment. Most people since they can't see anything in the water don't want to hear about the pollution. (I guess they figure if they don't know about it, it will go away in time.) But each year it gets harder and harder to remove the waste material from the water you drink. It naturally gets more expensive too.

This same pollution kills small, sometimes microscopic, life forms, animal and plant, in the streams and oceans. These are some of the basic raw materials for producing food at the bottom of the food chain. These small forms also produce most of our oxygen for life forms to breathe. Food and oxygen that we at the top of the food chain depend on for life.

At one time it was believed that the oceans were so big that there was no way that they could become polluted. Cities along the coastlines of the world pumped their liquefied wastes directly into the oceans without any kind of treatment. They hauled their more solid waste material and trash in barges farther out into the ocean and dumped the stuff far enough away from the coast that it surely wouldn't do any harm. That waste material has begun to get concentrated enough now to kill the life in the oceans near the shores. You read of fish kills where millions of fish die and wash up on the beach, causing a great stink, both economically and physically. This is sometimes due to the wastes causing a rapid growth of certain kinds of organisms that are harmful to the other life forms around it. There are also instances where solid wastes of all kinds are washing up on the beach, making it dangerous to even walk along the beach. Surprising as it might be, the oceans are not totally filled up with living creatures. Much of the deep ocean has very little life of productive value. Only in certain areas of the ocean can the light penetrate well enough to produce food and oxygen. If those areas of production are becoming so polluted as to cease production, it's just one more step closer to chaos.

Now that's just the waste material from our homes. It doesn't include atomic wastes or industrial wastes, which are another dimension of the problem even worse than the first. It's interesting to note that the United States is receiving hundreds of tons of radioactive wastes in the form of spent fuel rods from nuclear reactors overseas. We have a hard time figuring out what to do with our own atomic wastes, yet it seems we had agreed to take and store the atomic wastes from Europe's plants. (To keep the stuff from being used as materials for atomic bombs. A good thought but still a big waste problem that is going to get bigger. Besides, doesn't every nation in Europe the size of a postage stamp already have atomic bombs?)

So what does pollution have to do with violence? First it's going to have an effect on food production and possibly on oxygen production. The food problem would show up sooner than that of oxygen. We've already gone over what can happen as far as violence is concerned if food gets short worldwide. Couple that with the diseases that could become common when pollution gets real bad, plus the psychological effect of living in a garbage heap. Even some nice people might get mean. Pollution will fit right into the pattern of violence to come.

And now the raw materials. Inexhaustible? That's a laugh, even though the world acts as though all of our raw materials are infinite. How many oil wells have you seen that are no longer working? Pumped out. Empty. There are many of them in this part of the country. How about coal mines? There are many good fishing holes now where there used to be veins of coal.

The raw materials of the world are not inexhaustible, yet we use them as though they will never run out. Our forests, which produce our lumber, paper, and other wood products, are supposed to be a renewable resource, yet they are being destroyed at a fantastic rate. Still the fat lumber barons sit back and gloat, "We've cut 100,000 trees this year but we've planted back 110,000 trees to replace them." Hot dog! Those six inch seedlings they planted will grow to be trees, yes but not in our lifetime. A six-inch seedling doesn't remove nearly as much carbon dioxide from the air or put as much oxygen back into the air as a full-grown tree either. You say you haven't noticed any difference in the air quality? You will. It takes time. The quality of life will not degenerate over night, but may be gradual enough that they aren't even noticed until it's a little too late. You may not even notice until you have to start lugging a bottle of oxygen around on your back.

There are many other aspects of this, all tied together, the pollution, the food, wastes, raw materials, and so on. You can't separate them. They are subjects that are interrelated. One gets out of kilter and they all get more or less out of kilter.

Now what does all this have to do with violence in the world today? I'm saying that as these problems that I've mentioned become more pronounced, the violence is going to get more pronounced-more violent. Even now, look at some of the nations that have food and water shortages, lack of raw materials, pollution problems, etc., you will see much more violence as life is much less highly esteemed.

But enough of that for a moment. That's something for the future. Near future, true, but still in the future. Let's consider some of the reasons for violence today in our country. Since we seem to have plenty of food, plenty of room, plenty of raw materials, and so far, places to store our waste materials, why is there so much violence, especially in the United States today. (Though I think you'll find other parts of the world are even more violent than the United States, they just don't have a reporting system as efficient as ours.) (Oh the last couple of years our efficient reporting system tells us crime is going down, but when you read the newspaper you have to wonder where it's going down. Makes me wonder if the efficient reporting system might be fudging a little to make some grant giver think those federal grants are solving the problem of crime.)

I'll list what I consider to be the most obvious reasons for our violence, then go in to detail about each. Then we'll see if there might be a solution to the problem.

The breakdown of the home and family is tied for first place with the failure of the church. Alcohol and drugs are tied for second place. The criminal justice system and law enforcement are tied for third place. Let's have a fourth place winner in this contest. The educational system and television (or electronic gadgetry) could be tied for that fourth place. Trophies and awards to be presented later.

PS: The number of abortions has gone up to over thirty-five million since this book was started.

Chapter Two

The Family and Home Life

Let me preface this chapter on the family and home by saying there are many families that are very tight knit units. There are many homes where there are all the necessary ingredients for making a happy loving family. Most of these functional families and homes make very little stir as far as trouble or commotion is concerned, and yet members of those families often contribute a great deal to the community in which they live. Many of these families though not all by a long shot, are solid Christian families and nothing much will ever be able to break them up. There are also families where the parents try hard to guide their kids into the right paths, but it seems no matter how hard they try, the kids go their own way, often the wrong way. Some of these parents are part of Christian families, some are just good hard working non-Christians, and some are not Christian, not hard working, just caring people. I've seen all types pulling their hair out, as things seem to be going to Hades in a hand-basket, especially where their children were concerned.

These families, the solid families, the functional families, aren't the families we're primarily concerned with for this treatise.

Let's look at those families and homes that don't seem to stand a chance of making a go of it. That is something that seems to be happening more and more often in this age. Did you ever notice a couple getting married and say to yourself, "I wonder how long that marriage will last? I'll give them six months or a year at the most." It sometimes seems almost as though the people getting married aren't expecting the marriage to last very long either.

If you take a survey in almost any classroom in the United States you will find that a majority of the kids come from broken homes. Many of the kids have experienced two or more fathers before they reach their teens. Less common but happening more often is the family where the kids have lived through several "mothers", or stepmothers. Some of these kids don't really have any idea who their real father is and occasionally they don't know who their real mother is or was. Some have a home life so unstable they really don't know who they are, which leads to some real emotional problems. Couples living together without the benefits of being legally married have become so common that it is no longer something to even raise an eyebrow about. (I've heard it discussed as to whether another category should be added to application forms, single, married, divorced, live-in.) The basic unit of our civilization today is the family. A family consists, well, at one time it consisted of a father, a mother, and children. Today some people are trying to get it to consist of two males and kids, or two females and kids, or some other weird combination of characters. The United States can't claim to be the first nation to try to improve on the family plan of God, Rome was an empire that tried it two thousand years ago. Before Rome there were others but let's take a look for a moment at that ancient empire of Rome.

Rome was an empire that lasted as long or longer than any nation or kingdom ever lasted. It was the most powerful nation on earth for hundreds of years. In its beginning, Rome was built on the family unit. Keep in mind that since Rome lasted for about one thousand years, it lasted a lot longer than the two hundred plus years that the United States has been around.

In its beginning Rome was a very small nation. However its family units were very strong. The bonding, the unity, the loyalty between family members extremely cohesive. The family unit was headed by the father and though we would consider him too autocratic for today, he kept the family welded together very well. Things ran efficiently and smoothly on the farm, if somewhat legalistic and stuffy. This type of strong unity carried over into the government developed by the Romans until at the height of its glory there was no nation or kingdom that could stand against the might of Rome. The loyalty to the family carried over into total loyalty to the nation. By our standards the Romans were harsh and hard. He had a strong government, clear rigid laws, a well trained and disciplined army, and everything seemed to be going his way. But then things began to happen. As the empire conquered more territory, more nations, it became more and more prosperous. There were many more slaves brought in to do the work so there was much more time on the hands of the ruling classes. Some of these slaves that were brought into the empire brought with them some ideas, customs, and activities that were quite foreign to the old time Romans. For instance the Greeks brought with them not only art and literature, but homosexuality, sexual promiscuity, and new gods. This fit right in with the extra time the Romans had on their hands. Though wine had been around for a long time, with the extra time and bigger parties, there came to be a great deal more drinking. Combine all these things and the family was the first institution to bite the dust. Following the degeneration of the family there followed corruption in the government and degeneration of the same. As the government went downhill, the army became corrupt and began to degenerate. As the family units broke down in the empire of Rome, the nation of Rome began to break down. What was the most powerful nation on earth in its day, was weakened from within until it was defeated by barbarians. Barbarians that had far less to start with and yet they swept over Rome like a flood. Now let's look at us. (U.S., United States.)

You might say that true family life exists in only a few families and home life is also nearly non-existent. (Now you might not say that, but it doesn't make it so. Your family may be an exception and really be a close family with a great home life. It may also be that your head is in the sand. If your family is one of those exceptionally good ones you may be able to help others.)

Why has this tragedy happened to the American family and American home life? When did it all happen? Did it happen overnight?

The last question we can answer no to very quickly. It did not come about overnight. It came about in such a slow smooth manner that many had to wonder where they went to sleep to wake up in a different world. The changes were starting back some thirty, forty, or even fifty years ago. I taught school from the mid-fifties through the seventies in public schools, and the early eighties in a private school. It was easy to see the changes over a twenty six-year stretch.

In the 1950's and 1960's it seemed that parents felt whatever their child did was all right, as long as it didn't interfere with the Mamma and Papa thing. Mamma's and papa's thing might be visits to the local beer joint, or parties, or their work, or even their church activities. A generation grew up with no direction in their lives. No guidance. Just don't get in such trouble as will disturb Mamma and Papa. A part of this give them free reign philosophy also included wanting no one else to guide or correct their children. No one was supposed to find anything wrong with their little darlings, because their little darlings could do no wrong. If you found something wrong it was because you were doing something wrong. The bleeding heart Dr. Spocks of this world decided it would be better to gently lead the young people into the right paths even if the young people wanted to go off down a different path than what the parents might want. This, rather than give them firm guidance in the right direction, sometimes with discipline calculated to get their attention. (All too often the parents didn't know what was the right direction to begin with, seeing as some of them had never grown up. Many of those parents never became mature individuals, but continued in adult life just as they had in high school, being concerned with the one big aspect of their lives, to party, party, party. If the one big deal in your life is to party, then they couldn't see anything wrong with their children going after the same thing, unless their kids got into trouble. Then someone else must have fouled up. (Probably the police.)

The problem with those parents as well as Dr. Spock and company was they had no answers for when the kid didn't want to do what he or she should be doing. After all, to discipline them in such a manner as to force them to learn, or behave in a socially acceptable way, or even behave in a rational, safe and sane manner, might put a kink in their little egos. A whole generation of do-gooders swallowed this philosophy hook line and sinker. For many of those young people that have descended from those undisciplined parents it is now too late to do anything with them. They are too old to spank, and you can't lock them up, so the social worker just tears his or her hair out and hopes for the end of the day. (And the teacher who is supposed to be teaching said children just ignores the disrespect, the disruptions, tears his or her hair out and waits for the end of the day.)

The last few years have really been a time of change for young people. Many of them have really begun to realize that they can do about anything they want to do and nothing can be done about it, due to our bleeding heart laws and do-gooder social worker types. A mother called me up one morning while I was Chief of Police and asked if an officer could go by her home and make her son go to school. The school had called her at work and informed her that her son was not in school. I went to the home and found the boy, age 15, in bed. It took some door pounding to get him up, but he did finally get up and when I told him to get dressed he did so. In the patrol car on the way to school he asked me what would have happened if he had refused to get dressed and go to school. He didn't wait for me to answer, but told me that I couldn't have done anything, and that after he got to school if he wanted to he could just walk out and go back home to bed. He also advised me that there was nothing that I or his mother, (single parent) could do to make him do anything. I couldn't give him an argument, since I couldn't lock him up, that's against the law. There really wasn't anything I could do and he knew that as well as I. Oh, I did give him the routine talk about the need for an education to prepare him for life in the big world, etc. He didn't hear me. The do-gooders don't want you to discipline the children, but they don't have any answers either for when the child isn't as pliable as butter. Very few young people come under the heading of butter. Now we are trying to figure out ways to deal with the rebellious young people, but by the time they are teenagers it is a little late to be trying to put the brakes on them. That seems to be such a simple and obvious thing, I wonder why none of those highly paid social workers haven't figured it out yet. The training for later life has to come in the very early years. God, who created man, set up this policy for training the young several thousand years ago. But then I guess if you feel you have a better plan than God, you will abandon His plan and go for your own. That's man's plan. It hasn't worked yet, but there will always be the liberal type do-gooders that will try to play god.

I thought it interesting that only a couple of days ago, one of the psychologists came up with the startling conclusion that in the next few years teen crime, violent teen crime, is going to be the number one problem of the United States. Most law enforcement people could have told him that several years ago. Even more interesting was another program the same day where adults and teenagers were complaining about law enforcement using undercover officers to catch teenager drug pushers in high schools. That would be parents complaining along with their children that it was unfair to use undercover agents in high school to trap the drug pushers. I suppose the parent and their teens figured law enforcement should just get out of the way and let the teens do their drug thing. Perhaps they figured it would be better to have drug addicts running the halls than to have the teens put under the stress of wondering if they were talking to a law enforcement officer. They might not feel comfortable doing their drug thing.

There are many social workers whose job is paid for by the government, that insures that they will have that job until they are ready to retire by making sure parents are afraid to discipline their kids. This is even when the parents want to raise their children right. These social workers feel they are sharp enough to talk to the rebellious teenager and convince them to shape up and be a good kid and become a productive citizen. These teenagers are not dummies. They can figure out what the social worker wants to hear and butter them up enough that the social worker feels that he or she has accomplished a miracle with the subject.

I've talked to more than one parent that has told me they are afraid to discipline their children. They are afraid because an ex-husband, ex-wife, doting grandparent, or nosy neighbor will report them to the social worker as child abusers. Even some children are smart enough to report mom or dad if they get angry because they have been disciplined or if they have been refused something that they want. This means that these children are totally on their own. There are no reigns on them at all because the parents are afraid to do anything in the form of discipline. Keep in mind there is a difference between discipline and physical abuse. Unfortunately the bleeding hearts make no distinction between discipline and abuse. To them it is all abuse. Only gentle talking is allowed. Which means after the young person gets calluses on his or her eardrums they can do whatever they want to do.

Of course most parents want to discipline their children after they become teenagers and that's a losing battle. There is a saying, as the twig is bent, so grows the tree. Go out and look at some tiny seedlings. Those that will become mighty trees. You will find some that are crooked, bent, or deformed. Those seedlings or twigs will never grow into tall straight trees unless they can be from a very early stage be gradually bent or shaped into that straight form that will become a mighty tree. If you try to straighten up a tree that is six inches in diameter, you're going to have a monumental task, if it can be done at all. So it is with children. It is the gentle shaping, the teaching, the discipline, that is given to them in those first few years that determines how they are going to grow. That doesn't mean it can't be done later in life, as there are many notable exceptions whereby adults have made changes and become productive citizens.

One of the problems with family life today is the life style of the parents. Years ago the mother stayed home and raised the little ones while the father made the living, usually coming home each night after work to take care of the little problems that mother couldn't quite handle. Now I know those liberated mothers are going to yell they have as much right to be out there in the working world as the father. That's true. You have the right, but there is a price to pay. The price, in many instances, the loss of your kids. Many of the kids have been left to themselves or a baby sitter. Neither is qualified to be the parents. In many instances with both mother and father working there is no communication, no cohesion, no parenting for the children at all. Granted with the cost of things today in many families both parents have to work to put bread on the table for those kids. But kids still suffer from a kind of malnutrition. It's called parental care, or parental guidance, or just parental love. (There is a question too of is there a need for both parents to work, or is it just that there is the want for so many material things that both work to get those material things to the detriment of their kids. Or worse yet do both work to get away from the responsibility of raising the kids.)

Of course the left wingers have a solution for the children. Get them up at six in the morning, take them to a day care center where they are fed breakfast, dinner and maybe supper, then Mamma and Papa can pick them up at six in the evening, take them home and put them to bed. Unless Mamma and Papa want to go out on the town for the evening, then maybe the center can put them to bed there at the center and Mamma and Papa wouldn't have to bother with them at all. The center, government financed, would do this under the guise of making sure the children had adequate food and rest, so that they could grow up as healthy citizens. The powers that be could then train and raise up a generation of people that think just the way they want them to think. (They did that in Nazi Germany and in Communist Russia.)

When the family consists of father, mother, and kids, things can be rough, but when it consists of a single parent and kids, life can be a whole lot tougher. The one parent may have to work two jobs, or a job and school while trying to raise the kids, make a living, and prepare for a better vocation.

In any of these cases I've seen so many times when the parent or parents have had to just hope and trust that their teenagers, or seven-year-olds, or twelve year olds will grow up safely and productively, without the supervision, discipline, and training that they should have. Unfortunately hope and trust alone aren't enough in many cases. You read of many cases in the papers or see on TV news, where hope and trust didn't get the job done. What you don't read about or see on TV are the many times those parents get a phone call to leave work and come to the police station to get their son, daughter, or both. You don't read about the shop lifting, the beer parties, the sexcapades, and the run-a-ways because all that stuff is confidential since the kids are not adults. When the parents can't be in the home to raise the kids, they can't know what their kids do, and sometimes they hardly know who they are they know so little about them. I'm sure there are exceptions to this and there will be parents that feel their kids are exceptions. Question is, do you really know? Or are you speaking with your head in the sand? I've seen so many times where a kid or kids have been brought to the station after being caught shoplifting, burglarizing, DUI, or some other crime and when mamma or papa shows up they don't believe what's going on. In more than one instance the first words our are, "Why are you harassing my kid?" Sometimes it takes some doing to convince the parents that their angel has done something wrong. Sometimes they are never convinced, but are sure that the police just have it in for their kid. Meantime Jr. smiles and goes his way. I recall one young driver that miscalculated on fresh snow when trying to stop at a stop sign. She skidded, hit a utility pole, and drove on home. Now had she stopped, called the police as the law requires, the officer responding would not even have written a ticket, as he would have understood skidding on fresh snow. Leaving the scene of an accident he didn't understand and the inconsiderate officer tracked the offending car in the fresh snow right to its home. The parents were offended. It was harassment. It was not necessary. It was almost un-American. As far as I know the parents still feel the whole thing was the fault of the police. (I changed a few details of this incident to protect the guilty.)

Some place along here I need to mention those situations where the family is destroyed due to government help. If mother is alone with a bunch of kids to take care of, she can get some help from welfare. Now there are many instances where that help is a lifesaver. Mother just could not get by without it. It allows mother to take care of her children after father has been killed or has been taken off the scene for some reason. However, I know lots of cases where mother and father never get married for one reason. That is to get on welfare. The father lives at least part of the time, with the mother, but since she doesn't have a husband, she can draw on welfare. The father doesn't have to work, except to produce more kids, and the welfare checks keep them in beer and cigarettes. Not being married also makes it that much easier to change partners when life gets a little boring. Keeps the genes shuffled and everyone wondering who's sleeping with whom.

Then there are the violent homes. The homes where abuse abounds. I speak of three kinds of abuse here. Physical abuse, sexual abuse, and emotional abuse. Any of these forms of abuse in the home is enough to contribute to the breakup of the family unit and the promulgation of violence. In many homes physical abuse is rampant. This is nothing new. There have always been homes where there was physical abuse. There have always been homes where the father beat up on the wife or children, or the wife beat up on the husband or children. Sometimes it amounted to what we would call torture. But it is only within the past few years that it has begun to be reported and people are being arrested for doing some of the stuff that it is all coming to light.

When I speak of physical abuse I'm not speaking of a spanking of children when they need to be disciplined. (That's something that God ordained and I figure He knows what He's talking about, even if the social worker thinks he or she knows better.) I'm talking about the beating of wives, husbands, children, boyfriends, and girlfriends. Beatings that leave black eyes, split lips, broken teeth, bruises, cuts, broken bones, or even fatalities. Usually it's the man that does the abusing. He takes his frustrations, his failures, out on his wife, girlfriend, (that's his live-in), or his children. Or quite often it's the children of his wife or girlfriend and his is only the stepfather or step-live-in. Those that he abuses are usually too weak or too small to defend themselves. Occasionally the wife or girlfriend is afraid to speak up in defense because she is afraid he will walk out and she will have no means of supporting herself. (Now I have seen some men abused too, though not nearly as many as abused women.) Whoever does the abusing leaves much more than bruises or scars. The emotional scars that are produced often last more that a lifetime, carrying on into the next generation or even farther.

Quite often the violence takes place after the consumption of alcohol. I would go so far as to say that in ninety percent of the incidents of abuse, alcohol has a part to play. Other drugs enter in, in some cases, but alcohol is the usual drug of choice. It seems to release those inhibitions that keep the sober individual in control of his or her emotions.

Often the violence takes place in a fit of rage. Uncontrollable rage. I've seen the results of one gentleman coming home after a few beers, (just a few) and not liking what his other half, his live-in or love-in, had prepared for supper. He expressed his displeasure by knocking her against the dining room wall. It surely taught her how to prepare a different type of supper. Oh, he didn't have to eat the one she prepared as it was spread over the floor, walls, and ceiling of the kitchen and dining room. Another gentleman rearranged the face of his live-in because she wasn't quite ready for sex when he came in from the bar. Of course the split lip and black eye put her in a much more romantic mood. Or was it an erotic mood? Unfortunately for both of the above gentlemen there was no enjoying the fruits of their labors, as they both wound up in the slammer.

To be fair I must mention the gentlemen taken to the hospital to have his head sewn up after his wife struck him on top of the head with a heavy blunt instrument. She was in a rage. Now to be fair too, I must say she wasn't drinking, just in a rage. Rather uncontrolled as she smashed the furniture, dishes, etc., after taking care of hubby. The house inside looked like a party place for vandals. She later wound up in the slammer, but it did take some time to locate her after the incident.

Children watching the above kind of behavior, even if they are not a part of the abuse, are scared, traumatized, and grow up thinking that violence is the norm, and they in turn do the same things that they see their parents do. The children may start at a very early stage of life to act out this violence with other children, becoming more and more violent and uncontrollable as they get older.

Often the violence occurs in homes where one of the parents is a stepfather or stepmother. Since time began there have been jokes made of the wicked stepmother, but it does happen. The step one has no biological or in some cases no real emotional ties to his or her stepchildren so the abuse is easy to start. Once started it becomes more violent, more frequent, easier to trigger as time goes on. The perpetrator may actually resent the presence of the stepchildren and be trying to get rid of them, albeit sometimes unconsciously. This is not to say all step parents are bad, as many of them are loving parents that take care of their step children as though they were their own. In some instances they care for them better than the real parent would ever have done.

More states are coming up with laws that basically say, you do the abuse, you go to jail. So far, from the number of abusers that are being arrested, it doesn't seem to have stopped the process. When one victim calls for help and the perpetrator is locked up overnight, (which is usually the extent of the legal punishment), the couple often breaks up and the perpetrator gets another live-in to beat up for awhile. When the victim is a child the perpetrator of the abuse is given some counseling, which does very little good as it doesn't do any changing of the thinking patterns of the abuser. He or she only learns to say the things that the social workers want to hear them say.

Enough about physical abuse for the moment. Let's talk about another form of abuse that is popping up more and more and that's sexual abuse. You hear about it more and more, but I believe that it has been around for a long time. I believe sexual abuse was one of those family secrets hidden away in many a family closet along with other skeletons and only in the past few years has it become something that is brought out into the open for all to see. In some families that I have known, it is so ingrained that the children think it is the norm. The children then grow up to do the same thing to their children. Now the children are being taught to report any kind of sexual abuse to their teachers, doctors, or counselors, who by law must report it when there is probable cause to believe that it has happened. This means it is being reported much more often.

Again it is the male that usually is the perpetrator of sexual abuse, though not always. Alcohol is again often involved with this crime, though many kids are abused by close relatives, such as parents, grandparents, uncles, or other close acquaintances. Baby sitters or just friends of the family may be involved. A real potential situation is a live-in boy friend, alcohol and or drugs, and a little kid that is neglected. To be fair I have investigated a number of cases involving live-in boy friends, step fathers, and real fathers, as well as abuse by mothers.

Some of the abuses range from groping or feeling the kids to oral sex, to intercourse. Some of the abuses get caught up when a little kid makes some comment to a teacher or someone about something that happened to them and the report finally gets to the social worker, or to law enforcement. Sometimes the abuse goes on for years before the victim gets brave enough to tell someone what is happening. Sometimes the abuse goes on for years until the victim is old enough to leave home to go to college, get a job, or get married. After the victim leaves home and begins to think about younger sisters or brothers that may be going through the same thing that they went through, the older siblings make a belated report and investigation begins.

Whatever the form of sexual abuse that takes place in a home, the results can be devastating. The results may not be apparent at the first. There may be complications years later that will lead to the breakup of homes in the next generation or psychological problems that prevent an individual from having a normal family life. Even when the abuser is slick enough that the victim doesn't seem to mind the abuse, the damage will show up later. When families are broken up, homes destroyed, because of abuse that happened years before, there is often violence that accompanies that breakup. Because some of the parties will not understand what the underlying causes of the problems are, they get frustrated and the frustration leads to violence.

Emotional abuse is something much harder to detect. There isn't jail time for emotional abuse. You can't really even call the police to try to stop it. There are no physical scars, no bruises are visible, yet the damage can be just as devastating to the one emotionally abused. It can be something as simple as name-calling. When a child is put down long enough, told they are stupid, ugly, or any of many other demeaning terms, it has an effect. Many of the adults that we say have gone bad got that way by parents running them down to the extent that they had no self esteem. No self respect. They feel they are worthless and they usually become real problems of one form or another. The emotional abuse may be in the form of just ignoring a child, especially when there is another child that gets all the attention. It isn't hard to convince a little kid that they are dumb and ugly and that no one cares about them, especially when they have a smarter, better looking sibling that everyone makes over.

Emotional abuse often shows up by the child acting up. Some would say, he or she is just trying to get attention. Which may be true. But as time goes by and the emotional abuse continues, the attention getting may become more and more violent until the violence becomes uncontrollable. That's when law enforcement has to take a hand. Sometimes the results of attention getting may be called to the attention of law enforcement earlier if the child becomes a run-a-way, or does some vandalism or shoplifting. It can all be a prelude to violence.

A third type of home is the no parent home. Both parents work, leaving the kids to fend for themselves. The kids grow up, but they are shaped by and molded by their peers, by television, by their baby sitters, by who knows what. This is not to say that all homes are bad where both parents work in order to put food on the table. Some parents can even arrange it so that they both work and still have time with their kids. That's the exception rather than the rule though.

Many little ones grow up to school age knowing their baby sitter better than they do their mother. After all, when the baby sitter takes care of the wee one for six or eight hours per day, and the part of the day that the little one spends at home is sleeping, it stands to reason there would be much bonding with the baby sitter and ephemeral bonds with the parents. (If there were two parents)

In a single parent home and there are more and more of them today, the going gets even tougher. The single parent must work, if not on welfare, and that closes out any staggering of shifts to be with the kids. I've seen these homes where the father is the single parent and many more where the mother is the single parent. In some of these homes the parent really cared about what happened to their children, but the children were left alone too much of the time for the parent to have much influence on them. A couple of homes come to mind right off.

In one the father was the parent. He was taking care of several children and working a job that took him away from the home all day. I became acquainted with his nine-year-old son as a run-a-way. In the years that followed it was truancy, run-a-ways, shoplifting, vandalism, etc. Once I had to bodily pick him up and carry him downstairs from his bedroom screaming, when he was to go to counseling after he threatening his sisters with a knife. There came a time when the kid was so uncontrollable it was decided to put him in an institution for a while. It took three officers to put him in a caged car without damaging him. Each year the child gets more violent and harder to control. By the time he is eighteen he's going to be something else. His siblings have also been involved now in activities that show the results of being left to fend for themselves for eight to ten hours a day. The father of this family really wanted to raise his family right, but he had one strike against him when the mother abandoned the kids. The kids must have felt that they were not worth anything to begin with, then when left on their own for so much of the time, problems.

Another single parent home was one run by the mother. The mother worked eight to ten hours a day, leaving teen-age children to take care of themselves. She had to trust them to behave themselves. Unfortunately when they got bored vandalism was their thrill. They did quite a bit before they were finally caught. I can remember three incidents that they were involved with before the hammer fell.

That's just two of many. In both these examples the parents were pulling their hair out worrying about their kids and doing everything they could think of to make the kids behave. Unfortunately, in both these examples, it was or is too late. The twigs have already been bent. The trees have already grown to the place that only a miracle could or can change the direction of growth. The parents can only hope now that their kids will grow up, change, and somehow become productive members of society. What will probably happen though, is they will grow up and emulate their parents and produce more offspring exactly like themselves.

The family unit is the basic unit of our society. This unit is being broken down, slowly but surely, and as the year's pass it seems to be happening faster and faster. With the breakdown in the family and the feeling of not belonging to anything, or of not knowing who they are, the young of our nation are becoming more violent. More lost. More not caring what happens to them or anyone around them. As the family unit breaks down, our nation does likewise.

Chapter Three

Drug Abuse

One of the greatest contributing causes of crime, violence, death, destruction and confusion in the United States is drug abuse. Naturally we think of crack, crank, coke, meth, heroin, and some other such drug when we say drug abuse. All of the above are bad, but the biggest problem of drug abuse is alcohol. Oh, oh! Now I've made the bartenders, the brewers, and half the social drinkers in the United States mad at me. I can just see the gentleman at the end of the bar cussing and saying, "Two beers never hurt nobody." (I use the number two because that was always the number of brews the guys would admit to having when arrested for DUI. One of the questions always asked during the questioning after an arrest was "How many beers have you had tonight?" The answer was always, "A couple." Or "Two." It was never three or four. The next question was "Do you feel you can drive safely?" The answer was always, "Yes." This even though he or she may have been driving down the wrong side of the street while bouncing off the curbs on both sides of the street. It's always exciting to be driving down the street or highway and see a car coming at you in your lane. You know there is a problem somewhere and what do I do next. I've had it happen daytime and nighttime more than once while on patrol.

Since I've already mentioned alcohol a couple of times, let's take a look at it in greater detail. First, lets get it straight that I'm not a prohibitionist. Prohibition didn't work in the twenties and the prohibitionists didn't learn anything from that experience. I know of a lot of people that partake of alcohol in reasonable amounts and never have any problems with it or caused by it at all. Unfortunately there are hundreds of thousands of drinkers that feel they know what a reasonable amount is, but can't stop drinking when they reach that point, so they become problems.

Now those that sell the alcohol have a cause. It's called money. I was going to say greed, since it's the acquisition of money without considering the consequences of what will happen to others, but that wouldn't be nice to say something like that. They sell the booze to make money and they will defend the right to sell it and get their slice of the pie even if it kills everyone in the United States but them. They'll also say that if they don't sell it someone else will, so-they'll go ahead and sell it as a service to mankind. Some of them want even to expand their sales by selling to younger and younger clients. One bar owner tried to convince me that it would be a "good thing" if there were no age limit on who beer could be sold to. Her theory was that the fourteen, fifteen, or whatever year old kids were going to get it someplace, either at home or through friends, so why not let them come into her respectable establishment where it would be a safe environment to drink. People that drink and sell the drinks don't see any harm in it at all. (Or do they?)

The producers of the booze in their efforts to sell more booze whip out TV commercials showing beautiful girls and handsome young men, all smiling and having lots of nice clean fun. Not a bleary eye in the whole commercial. Not a stagger. Not a missed step in the dance routine. No one numb enough to ask the same question or make the same comment over and over and over. Not a single person so soused that they have peed their pants without knowing it. (A very common thing with heavy drinkers, both male and female. The people that make up the advertising haven't seen the real thing I guess.).

Cheers was an interesting television series. It was clean, quiet, humorous. I've been in a lot of bars and I can't remember any that look like the ones in the TV Commercials or for that matter I haven't seen any like Cheers either. Many of the customers, in real life, dark, smoky, bars, were bleary eyed, staggering, slurred of speech, but sloppily friendly, in other words, intoxicated or at least under the influence. Escaping from the world of reality. (It's called partying.) Now if they could escape reality and that would be the end of it, then that wouldn't be so bad, but if you watch the news, or especially if you happen to be in law enforcement, you can see that the escape is not for long and often leads to bigger problems than the ones they were trying to escape.

Take for instance car wrecks. Very few newspapers or television newscasts do you see that don't have something about someone having a wreck. Over half of those wrecks have alcohol involved. When you talk to those people that have been caught DUI, either because they were involved in an accident, or were arrested for some other traffic violation, you will find in nearly every instance the drunk driver does not feel it is his or her fault. It usually is the fault of the arresting officer, or at least the other driver, or a dog, or a deer, or even, as one young man told me, trying to avoid hitting a rabbit.

But the wrecks, violent as they may be and as destructive to life, families, and economics as they may be, are not the kind of violence that I am talking about when I speak of violence in the United States.

Let us talk about domestic violence. Domestic violence where hubby bashes wife until she is a bloody pulp and has to call for help. In nearly all of these cases one or both partners have been drinking. There are times when the violence is brought on by crack, crank, coke, meth, or some other drug, but by far the most common is alcohol. And beer is the most common way of ingesting the alcohol.

It doesn't seem to make any difference about the socio-economic status of the people. I've been called on incidents from a banker that chased his wife with a butcher knife around the house and over to the neighbors to the out of work laborer that used a shotgun on a friend living in the same household. Both incidents after having a few beers at the neighborhood bar, coming home and having a few words.

Most often the hand is the weapon of choice in these domestic violence disputes. But with a little alcohol and inhibitions dropping, the smallest difference leads to violence and any weapon that is handy will do. Bottles, pans, bats, even gumball machines have come into play. (I mean the heavy glass and metal gumball machine on a stand.)

And it isn't always the man that is doing the battering. I've seen some men in the emergency room with some pretty good gashes to be sewn up. The violence of one couple doesn't affect just those two people. Many times there are children. Always there are neighbors that get anxious. Each time it happens it seems those around just take it in and accept it until it is the norm for life. Children accept it as the way they should act when they grow up and the cycle repeats itself generation after generation.

Since the affects of wife abuse brought on by alcohol has already been discussed, we'll not repeat it here, but keep in mind that the wife is not the only person the drinking hubby bashes. He may take it out on the children if he can't reach the wife. (Or the wife may take it out on the children if she is the drinking abuser.)

None of these perpetrators of violence will admit that they are at fault or that they may have a problem, let alone admit that alky may be the problem. (After all, a man has to be a man to handle his booze like a man. Or a woman has to be a woman about her medicine.) It is always the fault of someone else. There is no accepting of responsibility with the drug abuser. As long as there is no accepting of responsibility, there can be no correction in life style.

Oh yes, occasionally someone with a drinking problem or a drug problem is forced to get some kind of treatment, or go to Alcoholics Anonymous meetings, or even spend some time in jail, but it does very little good over the long haul. Attending dozens of AA meetings, where a group of people with alcohol problems, or drug problems, sits around and tells each other how rotten they were, but how they beat the habit and now they are dry and/or clean. Not many of them stay dry or clean for very long. Oh some few get straight and don't get off the wagon again, but most will only stay dry as long as there is no stress or pressure put on them. No stress. No big problems. But when the stress comes, then there is the escape to the drugs or the bottle. Some go to jail. One gentleman, after being convicted of DUI the third time, spent ninety days in the slammer. Now you would think that ninety days would be enough to really dry you out. It took him thirty minutes to get home from the jail and thirty minutes to get loop legged drunk. I guess the jail time just made him thirsty rather than dry him out.

Some actually do get medical treatment. Some are forced to do things like go to the state hospital or some private institution if they can afford it, after they have had several DUI's or other incidents to get treatment and counseling. Too often what the institution offers for a cure is a couple of meetings with a doctor from Borneo or the jungles of South America. The doctor may have a degree in psychiatry but he or she may not be able to speak the English language well enough for a sober man to understand, let alone one with a drug problem. No never mind though, they can prescribe a pill for the alcoholic or the psychotic that will keep him or her calm and tranquil. Nonviolent. No sweat. (At least for as long as they remember to take their medication. Most of them decide they don't need the medication after a few days and they are back to square one.) Some of those doctors know even less about our culture, our customs, our problems, than they do of our language. How can they help? How can they understand the American mind, let alone the alcoholic American mind? I've seen very little help given over the years by this type of treatment. (OOPS! Now I've gone and slammed the psychiatrists and made them mad.)

Truly alcohol, meth, coke, etc., but especially that harmless stuff called beer, has had a devastating effect on American family life, on personal lives, on the economy. The average American doesn't realize the magnitude of this problem because most of the time they only read a few lines in the paper about Mr. X being arrested for battery on Mrs. X, or about the two car head on collision killing five people. They say about it, "What a shame." and go on about their lives. They aren't involved with legal processes, the broken homes, the damaged lives, the orphans left. (They pay for it in taxes, but that's hidden from them so it doesn't count)

Incidentally, I can't subscribe to that liberal theory that alcoholism or drug addition is a sickness or an inherited disease. I believe people get started drinking or using drugs for one reason or another, escape, relaxation, or whatever, then they use more and more until they become addicted, then they can't quit. It's like becoming addicted to smoking, only much harder to break the habit.

"But," you say, "You've not shown how this can be corrected." That's true. It was obvious that prohibition didn't get the job done. During prohibition there were the same problems and a law saying you couldn't drink didn't solve those problems. But there is a solution. You can't legislate morality, even though our government tries to do it constantly. Oh yes, there are laws against the use of meth and coke and other illegal drugs, which are good laws, but obviously the laws haven't stopped the use of those drugs. There is a way, however, to eliminate the problems brought on by alcohol or any other form of drug abuse. By doing so, many families can be stabilized the cost of health care lowered, the cost of insurance lowered, many needless deaths prevented, etc. I've seen drug abusers, such as alcoholics, meth users, coke users, paint sniffers, and others turned into sober productive citizens overnight. A big factor in stopping the violence in the United States could be achieved by getting a handle on the abuse of drugs.

See if you can spot the solution to this problem among these writings as you read along.

Chapter 4

Criminal Justice System

It has been said many times by many people, "There ain't no justice in this world." That sounds pretty drastic yet it sometimes seems that "there ain't no justice in our criminal justice system" and there are examples of the injustice appearing more and more often.

I'll divide the Criminal Justice System into three parts. First the prosecutors, second the judicial system consisting of the judges, and third the system of punishment.

The prosecutors, sometimes called District Attorneys, County Attorneys, City Attorneys, or just Prosecuting Attorneys, are lawyers that have the special task of filing criminal cases in court. As a prosecutor they don't file any cases that are called civil cases. (A civil case is one where no crime is involved, someone sues someone for money or some material gain. A criminal case has to involve some kind of crime.) Only criminal cases do the prosecutors work with. (In small governmental units a prosecutor may have a private practice and may take on some civil cases as a private attorney. If the district the prosecutor serves is of any size, the prosecutor probably won't have any time for private practice.)

Now let's see of what the prosecutors job consists. A person is arrested by a policeman, sheriff, highway patrolman, or some other law enforcement unit and charged with a crime. It could be murder, robbery, theft, DUI, or felony spitting on the sidewalk. The task of the law enforcement officer is to make the arrest, collect the evidence, write it all up and present the case to the prosecutor. The person that has committed the crime, or is alleged to have committed a crime, is often out on the streets on bail or bond committing more crimes before the paper work even gets to the prosecutor. (After all the person charged is going to have to have money to pay fines, lawyers, etc., so you can't deny him or her the right to earn their money.) Be that as it may be the prosecutor reads the charges, notes the evidence and it is then his or her job to decide whether to file the case or not.

The prosecutor has much leeway in whether he or she will file a case. If the prosecutor thinks there's not enough evidence to win the case, he may not even file.

There are other reasons they may not file, such as thinking he might just chew out the perpetrator and he will be a good boy from then on. Or maybe the perpetrator is a friend of the prosecutor, such as his mother-in-law. Or maybe the prosecutor doesn't like the officer that made the arrest. Now not all prosecutors are this way. Some are real go getters that really try to put the bad guys away and try to give a break to the ones that learn their lesson fast. I've seen all types. I'll give you a few examples as I go along.

If the prosecutor files the case, it is his or her job to prosecute the case in the appropriate court.

According to what I've been told by prosecutors from years ago, they liked a good fight. When a suspect was charged the prosecutor prosecuted. Not so today. Many of the people charged with crimes never go to court today. There isn't anything filed on them at all. Take for instance Domestic Violence. I've seen numerous girls beaten black and blue by their boyfriends, seen the boyfriend arrested for battery, put in jail overnight, released the next day after telling the prosecutor, "I'll never do it again." No charges of battery filed in court. What has been accomplished? The boyfriend was given a bunk for the night, away from his girlfriend at county expense. And true, he won't beat her up again, at least until he gets to drinking again. (Probably the next weekend.) It seems that alcohol, or pot, or meth, or whatever, has a tendency to make one forget little things like promises to prosecutors. The prosecutor does usually make the threat that if the perpetrator beats up his girlfriend again, he will file charges for the first and the second beating at the same time. He has two years to file a charge in most cases, though I've never seen them wait that long. In this age of fast food, fast bill paying, fast whatever, we have fast prosecuting. Better known as plea-bargaining.

In plea bargaining the suspect in a murder case pleads guilty to a lesser charge, say felony spitting on the sidewalk, and the murder charge is dropped or put on hold. Now it isn't quite that bad, but close.

For some prosecutors to prosecute the suspect in a case the suspect must have been caught in the act with a smoking gun in one hand and a written signed confession in the other hand. What I'm saying is the only way some will prosecute is when they have a case practically guaranteed to win. If there is the slightest possibility of an acquittal, then plea bargain.

Some prosecutors go so far as to select the cases that are of interest to them, whether they have merit or not and file on those while they dismiss or put on the shelf those cases that are less interesting. (Less interesting or less likely to make colorful favorable headlines.)

It is extremely demoralizing to law enforcement officers to do the very best they can in bringing charges on a suspect, then ten minutes before the trial begins there is a plea bargain reached between the prosecutor and the defense attorney. In this the suspect will usually plead guilty to a lesser charge and the rest of the charges are dismissed. Here is what usually happens.

A subject is caught after burglarizing a store. He is charged with burglary, theft, and criminal damage to property. (He broke the door to get into the store.) The burglary is a felony. You can do prison time for a felony. The theft, let's say was for less than five hundred dollars so it would be a misdemeanor. The criminal damage to property was also under five hundred dollars, so it's a misdemeanor. (You don't go to prison for misdemeanors, only the county jail for terms of less than one year.) The burglar agrees to plead guilty to theft and criminal damage to property if the burglary charge is dropped. The prosecutor agrees, and the burglar is found guilty of two misdemeanor charges. The burglar is sentenced to thirty days in jail, fined one hundred dollars, and ordered to pay for the damage to the door and court costs. The thirty-day jail sentence is suspended so the burglar can get the money for the fine, court costs, lawyer fees, and the door. The burglar doesn't go to jail at all then unless he spent a day or two there waiting for his trial. He is now free to go out and steal enough to pay his fines and court costs, and maybe the lawyer. The store owner will finally give up and pay for the damages to the door himself.

What has brought this kind of crap on? There are several factors that enter into the picture.

One is money. To the lawyer, time is money. It is much faster to plea bargain than it is to go to trial. If the prosecutor can save a day or a few hours by not going to trial, he can use that time to make more money. (This is primarily when the job is a part time job and the prosecutor has a private practice. It's all a part of the big picture. Meantime the defense attorney can tell his client, who he knows is as guilty as mud on a boot, "Well I got you off on most of the charges." He can feel good and his client has a sense of winning something, or getting away with something. A second factor is pride. The fear of losing a case. If the suspect pleads guilty to one charge, and the rest of the charges are dropped, then the prosecutor can chalk up another win for himself. (At least on paper.) He can go through life saying he never lost a case. That's good stuff if you have to run for office every few years. As for the suspect, he wins, since most of the charges are dropped and quite often he gets to plead to a lesser charge than the original one anyway.

One point for the prosecutor here is when the law enforcement arm of the system doesn't give him or her a good case, a strong case, then he may be able to salvage something by plea bargaining. Unfortunately law enforcement often gets the blame for not working a good case when it is only the laziness of the prosecutor that's to blame. For the most part the plea bargaining process is bad for the system. Too often it's, "You plead guilty and I'll not ask for jail time or just ask for the minimum."

Take something simple like a DUI. In many instances the drunken driver is arrested and charged with a number of crimes. If all the penalties were added up it would be much tougher on the drinking driver. But as it usually goes, after plea bargaining, all charges except the DUI are dropped, the subject gets the minimum sentence for the crime, and shortly he or she is back on the street, perhaps to be arrested next time after getting drunk, having a wreck, and killing some innocent citizen. The killing of some innocent citizen doesn't begin to tell of the devastation in lives and property that that one drunk driver causes, yet very little thought is given to that end of the picture, just make it as easy on the drunk driver as possible so that he'll plead guilty and make it easier on the prosecutor. (Besides, some of those drunks are important citizens that are too high on the social ladder to really prosecute to the fullest.)

There are a few prosecutors that can plead ignorance and get away with not prosecuting. It is true that a few lack enough knowledge of the law and the court system to get a conviction on a suspect that jumps up and down in the courtroom screaming, "I'm guilty! I'm guilty!" Hopefully as they gain experience they will improve.

And there are a few that are just plain lazy. Too lazy to prepare cases until it is too late. Too lazy to check out previous similar cases. Taking the plea bargain route is an easy way out. Then to fold the hands and sleep awhile.

I realize that many prosecutors have very heavy workloads and just don't have the time to give each case the full attention it deserves, but the system needs to be fixed so that the prosecutor has the time and the help needed to prosecute cases. The victims of crimes deserve that much consideration. The victim may be only the victim of the theft or a simple battery, but to him or her, it's about the most important thing in the world at the time. When the prosecutor doesn't even give the case the attention of filing a charge, the victim loses faith in the system of justice very quickly.

Oh yes! There is another tool that began to pop up once in a while a few years ago. It then became more and more frequent. That's the process called a diversion. Basically it's a means of buying your way out of a pickle. (Now I guess that wasn't a nice way of putting it. Sorry.) Diversion is a process by which a suspect pleads guilty to a crime, pays an extra heavy fine, a diversion fee, and promises not to do it again. It became popular when law enforcement began to crack down on drunk drivers. Some of the people arrested were people that weren't supposed to be arrested and heaven forbid that you should put some big shot in the slammer. Prosecutors like the diversion because they don't have to go to court and it brings in some money. (The diversion fee goes into a special fund of the prosecutors and he can use it for wonderful things like Law Books.) The diversion has grown up now and is being used for other crimes, misdemeanors, or infractions, such as speeding, head bashing, etc.

Now if you can get past the prosecutors to get justice, there is the hurdle of the judges. Between inept prosecutors and lenient judges you get disasters like the Stockton, California incident. In that incident a nutty sleaze went on to a school playground and killed five little kids with an assault rifle. Had the prosecutors been doing their job and the judges theirs, it would not have happened. The sleaze ball that did the killing had been arrested numerous times and should have been locked up tight in the slammer. He had been arrested for robbery, for drug crimes, and Federal laws concerning violation of firearm laws. But because of the liberal bleeding heart philosophy of the prosecutors and the judges, he wasn't locked up but turned loose to kill. Because of his record and because of his mental condition as noted by some of the law enforcement personnel, he should not even have been able to purchase a gun. After the shooting was there a big fuss about the lack of prosecution or lack of sentencing by some judge that took place before the shooting of the kids? Nay no nay. It was the assault weapon that got the blame. It was "Ban that terrible type of weapon that can walk onto a school playground and shoot kids." It might have been more worthwhile to ban the type of prosecutor and judge that allowed that gun to have legs to walk onto that school ground. It's interesting to note that there was practically nothing in the news media about the criminal history of this child-killing nut. It's too bad there can't be some form of assigning responsibility.

There are many judges that are good, knowledgeable, lawyer types that know the fine points of the law and are concerned with doing their part in meting out punishment to fit the crime. I've worked with several judges that were very conscientious about doing not only what the laws say, but in doing justice. They had compassion but stood for no nonsense. They were even confident enough in their decisions that they were not afraid to explain why they reached the decisions that they reached. That's a point that inspires confidence in the whole system, and it for sure inspired the law enforcement arm of the system. There are good judges, and then there are "other" judges.

Some of the "other" judges seem to feel that they are descendants of Judge Roy Bean of Texas fame. They make their own rules to suit the situation. They don't go by any law book and even worse, a decision given one week may be reversed for the next case, depending on who the defendant is, or how the golf game went, or which law enforcement officer made the arrest.

Some "other" judges seem to have a hatred, not for the criminal type, but for law enforcement. At least for certain officers or departments. When a case is brought before a judge that has it in for the particular department making the arrest, he or she will check every detail of the case and the first misspelled word, misplaced comma, or a flyspeck, they find in the paperwork, they throw the case out.

There are judges that have a bone to pick with the prosecutor too. When the prosecutor is presenting a case that the judge doesn't want him to win, the judge can say at the end of the case presentation, something like, "You didn't state what state the crime was committed in. Case dismissed." Now the prosecutor can't call the judge a liar. That would be contempt of court, so even though the lawyer or prosecutor is sure that he did state the location of the crime, since there is usually no record made of the proceedings unless it is a really big case, the lawyer will submit to the court. I've seen more than one prosecutor bite his or her tongue and watch their case go down the toilet because the judge had made up his mind before the case got underway that the defendant was going to be found not guilty, no matter what the evidence. You say it could happen the other way too. True, but it isn't often. The accused usually gets the break.

And what can be done? Nothing at the present. The judges are appointed and as long as they aren't arrested for some horrible crime, they have it made. Let me give you an example of how it works in Kansas. A judge is appointed to preside over say three counties. Counties A, B, and C. The judge does his thing in County A about ninety percent of the time. Now people in County A have him pegged for what he is, let's just say for instance, incompetence. Counties B and C have very little to do with him so they don't know anything about him. Now we get to vote on the judge every few years. The vote is just whether we would like to keep the judge on the bench or not. Sort of a vote of confidence. County A votes NO! But counties B and C, not knowing anything bad about the judge votes yes, we guess he or she is all right, might as well keep him or her on the bench for a few more years. The judge stays. It's a part of the system that stinks. If the people of three counties are going to vote on him or her, they should sit on the bench in all three counties equally. They all would know what that particular judge stands for and be able to make their feelings known. A judge should have a reputation that says to the people, either criminal or victim, prosecutor or law enforcement, you will get a fair hearing before this court. A judge should have compassion, but at the same time have a sense of justice being served.

Justice is perverted and the criminal laughs when the criminal knows that with enough money to get before a particular judge, he's going to walk free, or at least get a better deal, no matter how guilty he is. Is that any way to combat violence? I think not.

Last but not least is our system of punishment. It is said by some that punishment is not a deterrent to crime. It is said that the criminal type should be rehabilitated. Should be reeducated in such a way that he or she will become a productive unit of society. Now that sounds real nice. Those that espouse this bull have never been up against a rehabilitated mugger, robber, or rapist. They can spiel out this kind of philosophical drivel from their neat little offices without ever coming in contact with the people it affects. This philosophy is the culmination of the philosophy that helped us to get into the situation of violent behavior that the nation is in today.

Two generations ago, (maybe farther back than that even) the seeds of this philosophy were planted by mush headed individuals stating that it would damage the little egos of children if they were punished for doing something wrong. Since then those seeds have sprouted, the weeds have flourished, and a philosophy of non-punishment has blossomed into full bloom.

The law now is that a teacher or instructor can't touch a student, be they preschool or high school. It was the older kids that caught on first, then the knowledge trickled down to the four and five year olds. As one thirteen year old said to me not too long ago, "What can you do? You can't touch me. You can't lock me up. You can take me back to school, but I'll just walk away again." (This was the young man whose mother could not get him out of bed to go to school. I got him up and to school without physical violence, but what he said to me was the truth. Had he decided to stay in bed there really wouldn't have been much I could have done legally.) Now five or six year olds say to their teachers, "I don't have to do what you tell me. You can't make me." And the teacher for fear of getting involved with a lawsuit shrugs his or her shoulders and lets the kid have his way. (His way may have been bashing his or her classmates, destroying property, or just being a generally violent little monster.) Many of those same kids say the same thing, in the same disrespectful way, or even in stronger terms, to their parents.

I've had more than one parent tell me that they are afraid to discipline their children for fear of being turned in for child abuse. And for good reason. I know a number of parents that have been arrested for disciplining their children with an old-fashioned rod or belt. I know the children. They needed it. But now it's supposed to be just talk to them. Reason with them. Reason with the kids, and the kids get wilder, more violent. Yes, I know the reports tell us that juvenile crime is down. Maybe so, but it seems to me that I've heard of a lot of violence in the schools in the past few years. Much more violence that when I was in school anyway. Many of those children that need discipline will be those that are going to be so uncaring about life that they are arrested for crimes soon as they are old enough to be arrested.

But the do-gooder social worker screams, "Don't touch that child. Reason with them. Help them to understand." Perhaps that social worker could reason better with the child while the child is kicking them on the shins, stabbing them with scissors, or setting fire to their pants (that's unisex).

Those adults of today that grabbed on to the non-discipline form of philosophy as they grew up, in turn polished the philosophy until now they don't want even the hardened criminal to be punished, just reasoned with. Just rehabilitated. Just understood.

We hear more and more often of the "rehabilitated" criminal being released to make their contribution to society and that contribution turns out to be too often murder, rape, robbery, or such. Remember the Stockton, California shooting? I'm sure the powers that be figured that the killer would be a nice guy if they just let him go, after a counseling session of course.

How many innocent men, women, and children will have to be murdered, raped, or robbed before the bleeding hearts wake up to the fact that many of those criminals are much smarter than the bleeding hearts are? Many of those rehabilitated criminals have been sent to prison for just long enough for them to learn the latest methods in how to manipulate the system. They learn what to say to parole boards, probation officers, judges, and of course the social workers. They learn how to sound rehabilitated, even very religious sometimes, then as soon as they are out, some innocent gets hurt.

Now you can bet that the ones that get hurt aren't going to be the bleeding heart social workers or the probation officers, or whatever. No, they are well protected in their social shell. It will be the little guy that gets it in the neck. The store clerk, the waitress, the prostitute, the child, the little one on the social ladder. Maybe they aren't very high on the social ladder, but even the prostitute is a human being and doesn't deserve to be murdered, or robbed, or even raped.

And the hurt is not just the person murdered, robbed, or raped. Each of those victims has a family, or friends, or dreams. They have plans for the future no matter where they are on the social ladder. In many instances those dreams and plans are destroyed and only those close to the tragedy are effected and know the agony of the situation. The bleeding hearts sure don't know the pain and heartaches. They can say, "Well, the victim probably ask for it." Bull.

Punishment as it is presently meted out is not a deterrent to crime. It is only an inconvenience to the criminal. (And in some instances it isn't even an inconvenience. It is just a period of rest, relaxation, and a general recooping of the health of the convicted criminal at the taxpayer's expense.)

What ever happened to the idea that when you were convicted of a crime against the people of the state you lost your rights? Criminals are human, yes, but there has been so much bleeding heart bellering about the rights of poor imprisoned criminals that society has forgotten the broken hearts of innocent people whose loved ones have been murdered. The loud squalling of the civil liberties union has drowned out the agonized moaning of the rape victim. And no one feels the pain of the victim of the theft or vandalization when a lifetime of belongings and personal treasures are stolen or destroyed.

True, punishment is not a deterrent to crime when it is a slap on the writs and a scolding, "Naughty, naughty." But if the punishment were truly punishment it would make a difference. (I can hear the bleeding hearts gasping and murmuring, "Barbarian!")

If a criminal has been convicted of a crime and lost his or her rights and has been locked up, why should they eat better than the average citizens that works for the food on his table. They not only eat better but they bring lawsuits against the states if the food is not just the right temperature or seasoned just to their liking. (And there are judges foolish enough to spend time listening to their frivolous lawsuits.)

Why should the prisoners have the best that TV can offer? In some lockup the prisoners are forced to eat steaks and watch cable TV all day. Terrible! Terrible!

Why should imprisoned criminals have the privilege of hours upon hours of daily body building workouts to build muscles so that when they get out it will be easier to kill, rape, or rob? The body building also makes it more difficult for an officer to control them when they do get out and get caught in their next crime. It often results in the arresting officer getting seriously injured.

Prison should not be something that is just an inconvenience. It sure should not be a stay in the country club. I've had criminals tell me they wanted to go back to the slammer for some rest and relaxation. (Others have told me they could get anything in prison they got on the outside, such as drugs, etc.) When punishment is made to be punishment something that the criminal type does not want to experience a second time, it can be a deterrent. Maybe not a total solution to crime and violence, but at least a deterrent.

There might be some changes too, if the bleeding hearts could get it through their thick skulls that there are some child molesters, some rapists, some murderers, that are not going to be rehabilitated. To release them is to condemn some child, some man, some woman to pain, to perhaps years of terrible memories or perhaps death.

If the agony of the victims could be put on tape and the judges or parole boards or bleeding hearts that released the perpetrator be forced to listen to the cries of the molested child, the screams of the rape victim, the pleading of the murder victim, perhaps minds might be changed. (Or would they just say, "They must have asked for it.")

One thing that can be said for the death penalty, it might not be a deterrent to crime in general, but when a killer is put to death, it sure does deter his or her criminal career. (Even the death penalty has been so drawn out by bleeding hearts that it is a joke. It takes so long to get a murderer put to death for murder he's ready to die of old age before they push the button.)

Our criminal justice system has done much toward making our nation a more violent nation.

Chapter Five

Law Enforcement

Now since I've been in law enforcement, you will expect me to find no fault in law enforcement. Wrong, unfortunately, wrong. For the most part law enforcement does the best they can do. Whether you are talking about a Town Marshall, City Police, Sheriff Department, Highway Patrol, State Police, FBI, US Marshals, or what have you. Some of these organizations or units of organizations are excellent. They do their job in a professional manner that would make any group proud. Not all units or organizations can be proud of their accomplishments however. All of these arms of the law are made up of people, however, and when you deal with people, you have different ideas, different temperaments, different philosophies, just different personalities. There are elements in law enforcement that sometimes contributes to violence. Sometimes the contribution is done in an unknowing manner, but that's no excuse.

Basically there are three types of law enforcement officers, no matter what branch of law enforcement they are a part of. The vast majority are hard working, serious minded, mature type individuals that want to fight crime, punish criminals, and help people when there is need of help. Most are willing to go that extra mile to serve, protect, or assist. Many of these are extremely intelligent, highly motivated, and productive men and women that would succeed at any occupation they chose, but because they love law enforcement, it is their life. In many instances these people put up with low wages, poor equipment, and lots of bull from different sources just so they can feel that they are making a difference. This type of officer you'll find bothering their chief to go to extra training courses, even if it means doing it on their own time. They constantly try to improve themselves and become better law enforcement officers. The other day some researcher came up with the theory that most law enforcement officers were of the lower mentality types. He figured that people with higher mental capacities got bored quickly and left the profession before they had much chance to improve it. That might have been true some fifty years ago or even twenty-five years ago, but it isn't true for today. My experience today is that law enforcement is just about like the population. There are some dummies and some sharpies with a lot of in betweens. It seems that applicants for law enforcement positions are tending more and more to be better educated and more on the smarter side. In this age of computers, tangled laws, and lawyers seeking whom they may sue the dumb cop doesn't have much of a chance to get by. And as for getting bored-I found there weren't many times for getting bored. Would it be boring to be speeding across the county at ninety plus miles per hour to a big beer party where several hundred people were about to be invaded by several car loads of punks from a neighboring county, with fight on their minds. And you and one untrained reserve officer were the only law enforcement available in the county. It isn't boring.

Then there is a second type of law enforcement officer. I've seen them in every field of enforcement. They may be just as smart, or they may be not as smart, and they may be just a tad on the lazy side. He or she gets their job done, but mechanically, it's a job only. They never show any real initiative toward improving life, making laws enforcement better, more efficient, or doing any changing that they don't have to do. They are satisfied to drive around, swig their coffee, get a little lady's cat out of a tree, shoot the bull, and clock out. Nothing changes for them and they don't want any changes. Good old boys, but the criminals have their number and they laugh.

For these officers to do anything beyond what is outlined in the job description is unthinkable. Even training comes under this heading. If they don't have to train, they don't. Practical training, such as hand-to-hand combat, handcuffing, shooting, etc., they do only what is required.

The thought of taking a class on their own to improve their performance and chances of living is totally foreign to them. The idea of keeping in shape in order to perform what moves they do know is also foreign. Many of those officers get so overweight and out of shape that any little run or tussle is enough to get them exhausted if not in danger of a heart attack. The jokes about the overweight policeman and his donuts is not a joke. It may not be donuts, but there are plenty of foods around that are fattening enough. This kind of officer is just the opposite of one young officer I remember. He was a Highway Patrol trooper, patrolling out in the county. He stopped a drunk driver on a lonely county road. I was in the area and went to back up the trooper. The drunk driver decided he wasn't going to get out of the vehicle he had been driving. He was about a two hundred forty pound character with a reputation for being a scrapper. I arrived on the scene as the trooper asked the man to step out of his vehicle. The man said, "You're not big enough to get me out." (The trooper probably weighted one hundred eighty or ninety.) The trooper went around to the passenger side of the pickup, opened the door reached in and yanked the drunk out of the vehicle, and before the drunk could do anything, he was lying on the shoulder of the road, handcuffed. Three minutes later he was stashed in the patrol car ready to go to jail. The trooper wasn't even out of breath. That trooper was not only trained, but he worked with the weights on his own time so that he would have what it took to get the job done. But you don't find a lot of officers that are willing to go that extra mile on their own to be ready for that emergency.

In this second group of officers you could also include those that somehow wound up in law enforcement even though they are afraid of the people they are supposed to enforce laws upon. As long as they don't see anything happening or do anything, maybe they can get to the end of their shift without having to face up to any problems. These officers can drive right by a fight, fire, or screaming shopkeeper and looking straight ahead never see a thing before the next coffee break. Paperwork is also good to pass the time away without getting out and getting involved. After all the next shift has some officers that like to handle problems. Admittedly, some of the situations that an officer has to get into are pretty scary, like odds of a hundred to one, but if the officer represents the law, then he has no choice but to enforce the law. If he or she is afraid to do it, then they are in the wrong profession. When an officer is afraid of the people he or she is supposed to enforce law upon, it sometimes leads to violence, like having to use more force than would ordinarily be used, even to the point of shots being fired or other extreme measures. When a confident officer is confronted with the same problem he or she can usually handle the situation more coolly, and with less violence.

The third type of law enforcement officer is the one that usually causes the problems. Now let's not say they cause all the problems, since all law enforcement officers are human and many can make mistakes, or can be pushed into doing something that they are sorry for later. Sometimes when dealing with people that will not listen to reason, belligerent people, people on chemical highs, etc., it's possible for the best of officers to lose their temper or I should say, lose their cool.

The third type officer is the type that pins on the badge and buckles on the gun and becomes god. At least in their own eyes they are gods. They become insolent creatures that listen to no explanations, no reasons, they see only what they want to see and nothing more. If the suspected perpetrator of a crime wants to argue it's the cuffs, a baton, or worse. They feel they can do no wrong. To make it worse they get it in for certain people, or a certain type of person, a certain race, or ethnic group, and watch or follow those people until they make a wrong move, then wham! These law enforcement officers often push the people they don't like into a corner and violence happens. Violence that would not have happened if the law enforcement officer had been a real professional type.

Why can't that third type be weeded out? Up until now the answer was money. You couldn't afford to spend the money to find out what kind of officer a person was going to make after being hired. A few years ago many officers went through no screening process at all before being hired. I recall in one organization a person walked in to the head honcho's office, gave his name and said he was a Vietnam vet and was looking for a job. The man was hired on the spot with not another question asked of him. No background check of any kind was made, either local or national. A little local checking would have turned up that he had a drinking problem that did cause some problems later on. The first the head of the department knew of the problem was when the officer, while assisting at the site of an accident made a comment about himself being the town drunk. The department head looked puzzled and asked me, "What did he mean by that?" In some small department things like that do happen.

We now have psychological tests that give a very good idea of how an officer is going to act in stressful situations. These tests show how they will feel about their profession and even whether they should be in law enforcement or not. In some states the law is that any prospective law enforcement officer must take this test before becoming a certified law enforcement officer. In my state they have to take the test before going to the Kansas Law Enforcement Training Center. However, if you have a position open in a department, and ten applicants show up for that position, it's pretty expensive to give an eighty dollar test to all ten of them. What usually happens is one of the applicants is chosen, hired, and later before he or she goes to the training center the test is given to them. If the test says they are not cut out to be law enforcement officers, it's a little late to do much about it, since they may have been working as such for a year or more. With the labor laws the way they are it's harder to fire an unfit officer than it is to pull teeth. In the times that I've been through the process of hiring, I've been amazed at how accurate the results of the tests are. They prophesy the future behavior of an officer very accurately. As time goes by and the law suits mount up I believe it will be much cheaper to spend the money for the tests at the very beginning and try to keep some out that shouldn't be in law enforcement.

Now in larger departments, say ones that have thousands of officers, there are going to be bad apples in the bunch no matter how hard you work to cull them out. Take a department that has twenty-five thousand officers in it. There are going to be some officers that are not cut out to be law enforcement officers. No matter how many tests you give, there will be a few that can pass the test and get in. There will be some too that start out all right, but as the years go by they turn sour. Again to get these out of the profession is almost impossible. They have to really foul up to get bad enough evaluations to get the machinery rolling to get them out.

These officers usually have two sides. When a superior officer is present they can be as calm and professional as any officer. But out on their own, they make their own rules, their own laws, and heaven help you if your are on their list. The rash of incidents caught on videotape in the last few years, should give you an idea of how the bad apples act. Very seldom does the actions of a good cop or law enforcement officer I should say, make the evening news, even though there are plenty of tapes on the good guys. It's the video of the bad apple bashing a suspect, dragging a woman out of a vehicle stopped for speeding, screaming racial slurs, and a few other nasty things that make the evening news.

Law enforcement is changing. Part of the change has been brought on by things like the Rodney King case and other incidents that have gotten wide publicity. Part of the change has been brought on by departments wanting to be more professional, get better cases to the prosecutors, become better public servants. It is becoming a profession.

As the actions of the criminal element become more and more violent, it will take a better trained, more confident type of law enforcement officer to handle the situations. If the law enforcement officer doesn't handle the situation correctly, it will lead to more violence resulting in more serious consequences for both sides.

Good officers using good professional techniques can really help to keep the peace. (That's why they used to be called Peace Officers.) Bad officers tend to promote bad feelings, hatred, disrespect, and all together increase the possibility of violence. Violence in the form of assaults, batteries, criminal damage to property and other uncool things.

Chapter Six

Public Educational System

It wouldn't do to get through this discourse without mentioning our public school systems. I taught in the public schools for twenty-three years and in a private school for three before going into law enforcement. With twenty-six years of experience in schools I've seen a lot of changes. In those years of public school I watched two generations go through. From 1955 until 1979 I saw many changes take place, in the students, the teachers, the teaching, and in the parents. It was totally different in 1979 than when I started teaching in 1955. From what I saw while in law enforcement it is totally different now than in 1979. (For some real differences one could compare the educational systems of the 1940's with today's educational systems.)

Developing self-esteem seems to be the most important thing in the educational system. It is true that some students need some self-esteem, but to make self-esteem the god of education is somewhat too much. Many of the students that I came in contact with had more self-esteem than most adults. Some of them thought themselves totally invincible, totally "I can do anything, anytime, anywhere, and nothing can touch me." Self-esteem is something that every man, woman and child should have. When a kid grows up in a broken home where he or she is not sure who is going to be papa or mamma this month and to try to stay out of the way and be as inconspicuous as possible is not the way self esteem is built up. The kid begins to feel alone, lost, unloved.

But when the school takes over and tries to build self-esteem by lowering standards to the place where everyone makes the grade, where even the one with the sixty-five IQ. makes the honor roll. This creates a problem.

The problem surfaces when it turns out that American students come up in the bottom twenty percent of the world survey taken in 1997. That means eighty percent of students tested in this world-testing program were above American kids. Is it any wonder that when you go to the hospital you'll probably be treated by a foreign doctor? (I took quite a number of people to our state mental institution for examination and or treatment when in law enforcement. Most of the psychiatrists that I turned clients over to were foreign doctors. Some I could hardly understand their English. I guess they made the grade though.)

Now don't get me wrong. There are students today that are excellent achievers, as well as teachers that are excellent, but that isn't the norm. Many of the young people of today that would be excellent students don't have the chance to develop to their full potential for a multitude of reasons. We'll touch on some of them.

It is true that today our schools have many advantages that were not available thirty or forty years ago, such as computers, audiovisual equipment, laboratories, and so on. The curriculum has been expanded with different subjects until the offering is nearly twice as big as it was back then. But test scores show that the comprehension of math, reading, the English language, and other subjects has declined very much.

When I was teaching, (Science), I was disturbed by how my students could not read, spell, or write. (Some could. Some were very good at it. But many could not.) In the 1980's and 90's while in law enforcement, it was obvious in reading some of the statements and confessions, that many young people still could not read or write. Even simple statements were too much for some. (And that doesn't mean they were dumb, just that they had never learned to read or write.) And now a survey, taken overseas, says that kids in the United States ranked 18th in a group of 21 countries in Math and Science. As Mallard Fillmore says, "It could have been worse, there were no Asian countries participating in the survey."

Math and Science. Those are the subjects that the government spent millions of dollars on trying to improve forty years ago. Millions on training teachers in better and newer methods of teaching so that we could catch up with the Russians. Again, most of the money went to teachers to get doctors degrees so they could teach in college or get some higher paying job-but very little of it made much of a mark on the students that were supposed to be improved.

Not only had the three R's degenerated, but other things too had gone awry. Respect for the teachers, respect for authority was practically nonexistent. Morality had also degenerated. And obviously violence in the schools has increased. In the past few years the shootings are enough to make that known to everyone. The latest in Colorado being the worst yet. The government says violence in young people has decreased. Maybe so on paper, but it doesn't look that way in reality.

What happened? What happened to the educational system that was the best in the world? Many things happened. You can't put your finger on any one big thing, but there are many little things to consider.

It may have started with the parents. Parents too busy to pay much attention to what their kids were getting or not getting. Yet those same parents would scream bloody murder to the school board if their child didn't make the honor role or get on the team. Standards were lowered to make sure junior what's-his-name got high grades or made the team.

The teachers helped in this downward spiral. When the students who couldn't read or write went to college and got a teaching degree, they could only teach what they knew, which in some instances wasn't much. (Oh the Feds came up with a cure for that, money to send the poor teachers back to college, where they got higher degrees and started teaching in college, where they still couldn't read or write. But they did develop a philosophy colored by the Feds liberal left wing politics. Left wing liberalism. The college teachers then taught more teachers more left wing liberalism, plus teaching future newspaper writers, TV and radio commentators, and anyone else that would listen. As the teachers filtered back to the high schools and grade schools of the nation they began to spread the liberal crap that they had been taught.

Teachers at one time were looked up to-respected. Now you go into a school and you can't tell the teachers from the students. They dress like the students, they talk like the students, they sometimes smoke pot like the students, they pop pills like the students, some attend the same beer parties the students attend. As the respect for the teacher declined, discipline declined. With the decline of discipline, comes the increase in violence. Not a big change all at once, but slowly little by little the changes took place until there is the little problem of students carrying guns, knives, and other weapons to school, using them on other students and sometimes the teachers. (Oh! Excuse me. It's against the law for a student to take a gun to school. Ha. If you're going to violate a law by killing someone, what bother will another little violation like taking a gun to school matter?)

I remember when teachers started to really get with the liberal stuff when the National Education Association was really beginning to swing left. The local organizations began to act more like unions, getting rid of the old guard and pushing for a more unionized agenda. It was getting rid of the status quo, becoming more up to date, more democratic. But it didn't do anything for education, just increased teachers paychecks. Which is the main thrust of the National Education Association. They may talk about doing the right things for our children, but basically they are a lobbying union getting more pay for teachers. And they don't want any kind of accountability for their teachers either. Any kind of testing to see if a teacher can read, write, or teach, or have knowledge of his or her subject matter is meddling in a teachers private affairs.

Now that all sounds pretty rough on teachers so let me pour some oil on the water by saying I know some wonderful teachers that really try to give their students not only a good solid education, but even try to set examples for them as to what a good productive citizen should be. Teachers that are respected and looked up to by their students. Yet these teachers are often hampered by red tape and rules set up by the powers that be.

Drugs played a part in bringing down our educational system too. When drugs first started teachers really didn't recognize what was going on. Some of those pill-popping students that couldn't sit still, couldn't keep their mouths shut, were just thought to be hyperactive. Some of those pot smokers that could sleep through two or three classes quietly were thought to just have too much nightlife. It was only when a student was caught with the drugs that anything was done and that wasn't very often. When the good students failed ways were found to get them on through and when the poor or disruptive student failed, we sure didn't want them in class for another year, so ways were found to keep them moving through the system. It was only when the student began to get violent that he or she was really worried about. Little was done, some teachers were afraid, some too concerned with their own problems, and some were actually a part of the problem. I recall one sweep of the Jr/Sr High School, using drug-detecting dogs. There were three of us police and the dog handler. We got some mean looks from a few students as the dogs made the rounds sniffing at lockers, but most of the students were just curious, or amused. The dirtiest looks we got were from a couple of teachers. (One of which attended pot parties with some of the students.)

You've noticed the signs around schools that say, "Drug free/Gun free zone?" It isn't any wonder that many teachers are afraid to do much or to require very much out of their students when they don't know which ones may pull a gun or more likely a knife on them. With our bleeding heart liberals the way they are, if the teachers took the gun or knife away from a student and scratched or bruised the student in the process, the teachers would probably be arrested and charged with battery.

It's interesting that lately a couple of school systems out east are trying out a new philosophy. It is, if you fail, you flunk. Now that isn't exactly a new philosophy, but it is one that has been abandoned for forty or fifty years. It will be interesting to see how the parents of failed students take the policy, how the failed students react, and how the liberal do-gooders that fear for damaging the students' egos will take it.

Perhaps some school systems will even consider bringing back that old horror, corporal punishment, (Horror of horrors.) to help stop some of the violence, drugs, and all around nonsense going on in some schools under the name of modern education.

The educational system of America will have a long way to go however, before it can recover from the liberal ideas of some of our modern educators. Ideas such as there is no right or wrong, only what feels right for the time and the place. When you teach there is no right or wrong, then it isn't wrong to shoot someone, even a teacher. It isn't wrong under this philosophy to steal something, or to lie, or to cheat.

Yes, our schools have contributed to the atmosphere of violence that permeates our society today. When a student graduates or even before some of them graduate, some get the feeling or "What's the use?" They know they can't read or write, or that they aren't prepared for accomplishing anything in life, so what's the use in trying to do anything but party. Drink, puff pot, snort coke, shoot meth, and batter anyone that objects.

One other point on our school systems. I remember back in the sixties and seventies when the federal government was panicking about our failed educational system and began to try to raise the standards of education by pumping great squirts of money into it. They were trying to come up with some new method of teaching that would turn out geniuses by the truckload. What they came up with in subject after subject was, "Turn the students loose to learn on their own." Let the students expand their minds by exploring a subject on their own. This was really supposed to be hot stuff in science. What it actually was, was to let the students with no background in the subject goof off doing some lab work that they couldn't understand and wind up with no answers to anything. This even carried over into college teaching. Instead of professor teaching, the students were supposed to teach themselves and their classmates. The ignorant teaching the ignorant. This might be appropriate if the teacher didn't know how to teach or didn't know the subject to be taught. (Unfortunately this was too often the case in college, high school, and even grade school.) Too often in the field of science teachers would not have the right stuff for teaching science, so they would do only the experiments and exercises that seemed exciting, starting in the grade school. By the time the students reached high school some of those exciting experiments they had done five or six times. By then things were beginning to get a little boring. When things get boring, students get restless. Discipline gets harder to maintain. All this is just small steps toward losing respect for authority, toward escalating violence.

When you have fights every day in schools, when you have five to eight assaults on teachers per year in some large systems, when you have shootings and knifings, when you have rapes, I'd call that violence. Our educational system preparing our youth for a more violent future.

Chapter Seven

Gangs

When speaking of violence it wouldn't do to leave gangs out of the discussion. Years ago when one thought of gangs you thought of the Hell's Angels, the Bloods, the Crits, or a few of the older gangs, like the Jesse James Gang, the Daltons, or some that you've only seen in the movies. Now just about every city has several gangs and every small town has one or two gangs or at least a want-to-be gang. There are a lot of wan-a-bes. They often develop into full-blown gangs if not dealt with properly.

Why has the number of gangs increased by so many fold? Why are the members of these gangs so much younger than the gang members of old? And why are the members so much more prone to violence than the gangs of old? (Oh the old wild west gangs shot a lot of people in the line of work they were in, robbery, cattle rustling, etc., but they didn't usually just ride around shooting people just for the fun of it) And the more contemporary gangs, like the Hell's Angels did a lot of dirt, such as robbing, stealing, raping, drug running, and killing, but again it was sort of in their line of work. Generally they didn't kill you unless it was necessary.

Most of these questions can be answered with the chapters you've just read. But let's do a little reviewing, starting with the age of the new gang members. Teenagers down to ten or twelve year olds. (Some even younger in some places.) Why would a kid so young even consider joining up with a gang that commits acts of violence, does burglaries, robs, does drugs, and other unsavory things? The young person has a need. They are missing something in their lives and the gang presents the only way for some of them to find what they're looking for, or to fulfill the need that they feel in their lives. (That's a real black eye to parents, schools, churches, and any one else concerned.)

In many instances the kids have just been turned loose on the street, to get them out to the house and out from under foot. They are turned loose with no parental guidance, no teaching, no nothing. Just don't bother me. Just go away. If the kid comes home to go to bed, they know he or she is still alive, but what they've done all day is not known and not cared about. Some of those parents may still be getting welfare off of the kid that is roaming the street, though that is supposed to stop pretty soon. (We'll see. We'll see.) Most of these kids are not introduced to any form of religious training, though some get a little in their early years. Not enough to keep them from robbing, stealing, or killing. If they are on the street, they aren't in school, or at least not for long. This means they aren't prepared to take advantage of some opportunity in life if one should appear.

Some kids are not turned loose on the streets but kicked out of the nest to make it on their own. This kind of thing happens not only in the large cities, but even in small town USA. So what happens when these kids are more or less abandoned? They have a need. They have needs for the basic things of life, like food, clothing, and shelter. That's the short-range needs. But they also need to feel like they belong at least to something. They have a need to feel like somebody cares, that somebody loves them. That they are not alone in a very uncaring world. What would be more natural than for the kids to group together and support one another? By forming a gang they can belong. They can look out for one another. Naturally you're going to find in these groups someone that is dominant, either by age, size or street smarts, that will become the leader. He or she will become the father figure or the mother figure. There will be no love involved, only power. That leader will have the power to direct the members of the gang to do all kinds of things that a non-member would not think of doing.

There is another way that kids join gangs. In some areas the gangs are so strong that a kid is in mortal terror constantly unless he or she is a part of a gang. After all, it would not be much fun to get beaten up every time you stepped outside your home, or off the school ground, so for self-preservation, they join the gang.

Once a kid becomes a member of a gang there are certain things they have to do to prove themselves to the gang, or to advance in the hierarchy of the gang. This is like the old motorcycle gangs. They had or have a set of rules whereby you have to do certain things in order to be able to wear certain badges or insignia on their colors. (Coats or vests.) I won't go into the requirements for some of the patches as some of it gets a little nauseating. But if you see one of those members of a motorcycle gang with a lot of different colored little wings on his coat, you know he's been around.

With the kids, proving themselves might be stealing something, fighting, robbing, or even killing someone. This last is the cause of some of the drive-by shootings, a gang member proving that he has the macho to go the ultimate distance by killing a human being. (Although they don't always consider who they kill as human beings.) The girls are usually required to prove themselves by sexual acts, such as taking on all the male members of the gang in one orgy. However, this form of proving oneself may be changing to a more violent form of activity now, as girls seem to be getting more violent as the years go by.

A part of the proving, the activities required to be a real part of the gang, may be drug abuse. Alcohol, marijuana, coke, meth, pills of all kinds, and combinations of drugs may be abused. This in turn leads to more crimes, more violence, or deaths.

It's a little sad how some social workers feel that if you can just talk to gang members you can get them all straightened out. What do the social workers have to offer the gang member? Security? No. A feeling of belonging? No. A feeling that somebody cares? No. A little talking is not going to make up for a family with its parental love and guidance. A little talking isn't going to make up for what the church has failed to do. And a talk by the social worker isn't going to reach the whole gang.

There are hundreds of kids that are being reached by some organizations that give them the things they seek in the gang. But there are thousands of kids that are being shoved, pushed, or seduced into gangs, large and small.

The gang fulfills many needs in the life of the young boy or girl. It takes the place of parents for guidance, training, and loving care. It takes the place of the home for stability, security, and shelter. It takes the place of the church for goals and direction in life to the point of becoming the god of the young persons life. It becomes the reason for being for hundreds of thousands of young people. Young people that have no hope, no dreams, no concept of the future. Is it any wonder that when things turn violent the gang members do their violence without a second thought, without any thought of consequences? Life to them is very cheap. (And in other countries where life is even cheaper than in the United States, it gets worse.)

Chapter Eight

The Church

The entity that must assume most of or at least assume a huge portion of the blame for the mess we are in, is the church. I use the term church to mean religious organizations in general, not the true Body of Christ as the Bible describes the church.

Let me say to begin with, since I know I'm going to make a lot of people angry, that in every church or body of believers, there are good, God fearing, Christ loving, people. Even in the deadest of churches there are some real true Christians, living Christian lives, and trying always to please God. Some of these Christians are serving the only way they know how, and that's the way that they've been taught. There are many good hard working church members that have never had the experience of really knowing Jesus Christ. It reminds me of Martha, so busy in the kitchen, preparing tasty food for Jesus, that she was missing the part Mary was having, sitting at the feet of Jesus-listening to His words, absorbed in His teachings.

Martha was working her fingers to the bones trying to take care of all those details, material details, while she missed the most important part, the close relationship with Jesus. She knew Jesus, yes. She knew what He stood for and probably most of His teachings, but she was missing that intimate personal knowledge of her Lord. Many pillars of the church today are as Martha was, hard workers for the Lord, but without that personal intimate knowledge or relationship with Him.

I hope as you read this you'll keep an open mind and if someone sounds familiar to you, you'll not grind your teeth and burn the book, but do as the Bereans did, search the scriptures and see for yourself what God has in store.

Our country was founded on a basis of Christianity. Now obviously if you've read the writings of some of the fathers of our country it would be obvious that not all of them were practicing Christians. (One even rewrote the Bible to make it more to suit his tastes.) Nevertheless, the country started on a Christian footing. Family values were based on Christian values and this made for strong family ties. This got this country off to a flying start. It became the most advanced nation in the world.

Law and the criminal justice system was also based on Christian principles.

It is interesting that Rome, the nation that was probably the most powerful nation in the world in it's time, and lasted longer than we've been around, went through something similar. Rome's strongest asset was its strong family life in it's ascending years. As it began to take in Greek customs, such as homosexuality, free love, and a multitude of gods, family life went to nothing. The building blocks of the nation crumbled and the Roman Empire fell to a bunch of barbarian invaders, who had nothing like the Romans had with which to begin their reign.

Now how could a nation of so-called Christians, a nation that sent missionaries to all parts of the world sink to the place where missionaries would be called to come to America?

And how could I ask such a nasty question when there are so many churches all over the place?

Let me start by saying I'm not pointing at any church group, denomination, or class of churches. I speak of the church that is supposed to make up the body of Christ. Now that can be any of our Churches that claim the name of Jesus as their head.

There are all kinds of churches that claim to follow the teachings of Jesus Christ, but are nothing but dust in the wind. This should come as no surprise to anyone. Jesus himself said in the end times there would be many churches claiming His name, but without any power. Power that Jesus said those that believed on Him would have. But where is that power? Jesus healed the sick, raised the dead, performed miracles, and did many other things marvelous to behold, and He said those that believed on Him would do even greater things. Where are those that are doing even a small shadow of what the Lord said we would do-have we made Him out a liar? Out of the millions that go to church and call themselves Christians, how many are doing the things that Christ (that's where the name Christian came from) said they would be doing?

Let me say up front I know many people that attend church of one denomination or another, and are faithful, and are sincere, and are good people, but they fall far short of what God would have them be. Many fall so far short that their children see the fruitlessness of their parents, recognizing that they have missed something and the children try on their own to find the missing ingredient. They try to find it in alcohol, drugs, sex or violence. They don't find what they are looking for there either, but who is to guide them? Who is to show them what it is they search for? The preachers? Not hardly. Many of the preachers in modern churches don't believe that Jesus Christ is the Son of God and died on the cross to pay the price for our sins. Many of today's preachers believe that pastoring a church is a good source of a steady income without too much manual labor.

For parents, preachers, Christians, to fail to show young people the power of God, the love of God, or even to discourage the young from searching for a deeper walk with God is one of the most heartbreaking aspects of our modern society.

How did the church, especially in the U.S. get in such a pickle? Did it happen over night? Nay! No! It's taken nearly a century. Along about the First World War things began to go down hill. The roaring twenties really put the skids under it. Then the Second World War came along liberating more people, especially women, from the bondage of religion. After 1950 you could see a real stagnation of the church. The old folks holding on tightly, some of the young getting a spark occasionally, only to be stamped out quickly before any kind of wild fire got out of hand and upset the status quo. Someone once said, "Don't worry about the young people starting any spiritual fires in church, there are plenty of wet blankets around to put out any of the flames." Many members of churches are quite content to attend church once a week and sleep through a sermon, as long as it was not too loud or too disturbing.

As I think of Jesus, walking from one village to the next, hot, tired, thirsty, or cold, tired, hungry, teaching what the Father wanted of many, with no place to lay His head at night, I wonder if He does not sigh once in a while now as He watches what His followers have become, since His first followers who were willing to give up their lives to spread the Gospel of Jesus Christ. (Many of today's Christians won't even give up a TV program, let alone their lives for Christ.)

Where is the power that the church had, that Christians had, that would have held the last two or three generations that have been lost? The power is in Jesus Christ. Man has substituted man's gospel for that of Christ and once that's done, the power is no longer the Power of God that is demonstrated but the power of man. Man has demonstrated time and time again that when he, man, takes complete control, he fouls everything up.

Now that isn't what modern educators would teach. They'd say that man has within himself the power to become whatever he wants to be and to do whatever he wants to do. That's when God is put on a shelf and man becomes his own God. Didn't that happen a long time ago? Only it was Lucifer that tried to put God on the shelf and elevate himself above God- to make himself god. He didn't succeed, and man hasn't done any better at making himself god.

Here in the U.S. religious freedom and tolerance for all forms of religion is supposed to be the thing. This nation got a big boost to begin with by people that wanted to have freedom of religion. The feeling was so strong that it was even written into our constitution. The founding fathers wanted nothing about the government to interfere with the freedom to worship God. You say it's still that way? Nay, no, Nay. Since the secular humanist and the atheists squeal the loudest, religious freedoms are slowly being curtailed.

There will come a time when religion, the right to worship God will not be free. How can that possibly be you ask? Surely not in the U.S. of A.

While most church members sleep peacefully through that Sunday morning service, bothering no one, more active awake churches that see religious freedom slipping away are speaking out. As those churches speak out, they begin to disturb the powers that be and the squeeze begins to be put on them. Presently it is usually in the form of a financial squeeze, but in a number of instances it has been some small or obscure law or rule that has allowed the political hierarchy to close a few churches that speak out.

What could they speak out about that would upset anyone? Well, take something like abortion. That is a form of murder that is politically correct right now. Politically correct, but frowned upon by God. Now a church that is Godly correct has to speak what God says. If what God says is in opposition to what politics says, then those that are politically correct try to shut up the church. The result is persecution for those churches that would preach and teach the Word of God.

Take another political hot potato, homosexuality. It really shouldn't be political, but since the gay community squeals so loudly, it is political. It seems being gay is one of those politically correct things now. God, however, doesn't look at it that way. God considers being gay an abomination to Him. (An abomination means it really turns Him off.) Now if you wish to go to hell, or don't believe such a place exists, or don't care what happens to you after you kick the bucket, that's your business. You can be gay and God has nothing to do with you. Unfortunately gays want everyone to say, "you're all right." And maybe even join them. That's a little hard for God fearing people to do because it would be like, in the eyes of God, saying to a murderer, or a thief, or rapist, "that's all right, you're one of us." God says chose who you want to serve, Him or the gay community. But you can't be a part of both.

Since homosexuality is politically correct, then to speak God's feelings about it is to invite pressure by the politically correct to shut you up. You don't see much in the papers or on TV about churches being closed, but the news media for the most part is politically correct.

As long as a church, a body of church members, is sleeping peacefully, they don't bother anyone, especially the politically correct, and they can go on sleeping. As a matter of fact, some of those sleeping church members may even speak out against those radical religious fanatics that speak disparagingly against the gay community, or abortion. (As time goes by, and the sleeping members see that you get points by being on the side of the politically correct, they may even help to shut down and shut up those that would speak for God, or should I say, disturb their sleep.)

It isn't terribly hard for the politically correct to close down a ministry. The powers that be, using your tax dollars, can bring suit for trivial things and their highly paid lawyers can literally bankrupt a church in the court system.

The cause of our God has not been helped in the past few years by some of the con artists that have made their fortunes being TV evangelists. In all probability some of the failures didn't start out to be a con of the people for their money, but as the years went by and the money rolled in, that stack of gold became more tangible than the God they served. God was put on the shelf and the business of raising money became god. Then the business of fulfilling the desires of the flesh became god. Then the generations of young people looking for something to fill that empty spot that only God can fill, said, "if that's religion, it's not for me." They turned to drugs, sex, etc. Who can blame them? Did the older generation show them the true meaning of what Jesus Christ came to do? Not hardly. The older generations showed them the very selfishness that Jesus Christ came to do away with. And now the ultimate selfishness is being taught in our schools. Man is god. Do what feels good. There is no right or wrong, only feel good about yourself.

Even those churches that start fresh, with people making personal contacts and commitments to Jesus Christ seem to soon fall into the patterns of conformity. The struggle for money. The struggle to fill the pews. The struggle to keep that individual personal communication between member and God alive, gives way to the constant hassle to give, built, etc. (Martha, back busy in the kitchen.)

One of the saddest sights is to see a church begin on fire for the Lord, build a body of believers, experiencing the power of God at work in their lives-then the church shifts gears and goes into a neutral mode trying to hold on to what it had. (King Saul started out that way but he shifted gears, got out of God's will and spent the rest of his reign trying to hold on to his kingdom. He didn't succeed.) The congregation begins to drift away as the power drifts away. Then instead of reaching for the source of the power, God, through Jesus Christ, the church begins to try gimmicks to keep members in church and to add new members to replace those that are lost. If enough gimmicks are tried, raffles, bowling alleys, etc., etc., the church will just about hold on stagnant, but still there. The gimmicks are like applying ice packs and aspirin to someone with appendicitis. The aspirin eases the pain and the fever. The ice pack slows down the inflammation, but neither stops the appendicitis.

One popular gimmick is to try to instill new blood (and new money) into a code blue church by trying to make evangelists out of every church member. Only God can make an evangelist, yet preachers are constantly trying to do what God has not ordained. Paul said the body of Christ, the church, was made up of many parts. Each part with its particular function. Some preachers would try to have the body of Christ made up only of mouths. Now a big glob of mouths wouldn't get much done would they? Why not do it God's way? We Christians are to be witnesses for Christ, in deed and word and life, but we are not all evangelists.

The power that Jesus said the church would have comes from God. It comes from God through Jesus Christ, by the Holy Spirit. And it comes through individuals yielding themselves to God, communing with God, and receiving from Him. Then as a body of believers, all yielded to God, there is the power to do the miracles, healings, and other things that you saw in the early church. Then the young people could see that God is real.

That Jesus Christ His Son is real. That there is really something to religion besides a club to go to each Sunday morning. (Some even with coffee and donuts.)

There is a type of Christian that I call an exceptional Christian. They will tell you that they believe the Bible, except for certain passages. "Except for." Those two words make the exceptional Christians. They have decided that there are parts of God's Word that, one didn't come from God, or two, don't pertain to our times, or three, were a misinterpretation of what God intended. What they have actually done is set themselves up as gods, accepting the parts of the Bible that they are comfortable with, and discarding the rest. They have to justify their actions in some way because it would not sound very nice if they said, "I've set up my own religion and become my own god. I've elevated myself above God." Isn't that what Lucifer said?

There are churches that want to dominate the lives of its' members. Now you will immediately think of the Jim Jones thing down in Guyana. There you had total domination, even unto death, by one man. One man wanted to be god. He wanted total power over his followers. He wanted to fulfill all of his desires, his fantasies. He was totally selfish. His means of control was trickery, intimidation, and finally force. He actually started as a very personable individual until he had his flock so gaga over him that's when he began to go over the line, they followed until it was too late to turn back.

Now everyone says, "You couldn't get me hooked into an organization like that. Nobody could rook me into a ridiculous situation where I'd wind up committing suicide at the whim of the leader!" But nine hundred people did just that. Were they all totally insane? Nope. Just duped.

You wouldn't be duped like that, would you? Yet every day people are duped by religious leaders trying to exert control over their lives in much less obvious ways. They convince you that they are in direct communication with God and you had best do as God has told them to tell you. It may be in control of your money, your time, or your talents. Now God wants to be in control, yes. But His reasons for wanting to be in control are totally unselfish. He wants our lives to prosper and be full, but it is out of love that He has done for us what He has done. It is in love that He wants to control us. He would draw us with bands of love. That's the strongest tie that there can be. It is only out of love for Him that we can submit to God, knowing that He will do us no harm, that He will do the things He has promised for our good. He can only do this, as He is love. He never has a selfish motive when He wills for us to do a certain thing. He gave us a free will and to force us to do anything is totally against His nature. To force us through fear or anger, or need to bend to His will is not His way.

Speaking of fear it is interesting to think of the ways that some churches or preachers work for their flocks. So many are so very sincere, but so very far off the mark. Some try to scare the sinners in to being pious or holy by threatening them with hell, fire, and brimstone. Become holy or you will be punished. Now that works for awhile. The sinner is scared into repenting and lives a holy life for a few days, or weeks, or even years, then the fear wears off. Old habits sneak back in, and the individual drops out and is worse off than before because he doesn't want to get around any Christians that might scare him again. It reminds me of some of the law-breakers that I've arrested in the past. Take a drunk driver with his or her first arrest. Terrible, terrible. Scared. A horrible thing to go through. All that booking, jail, court, fines, embarrassment. They are cured! They will never do it again! They are scared. They stay sober-for awhile. But even though they know the penalty, as time goes by, the fear subsides, they begin to revert back to some of their old habits, then another arrest and the cycle repeats. The scare tactics works for a while but as time passes, fears pass. It takes more than fear to change the life of most people.

Then there is the gambit, "Do you have problems? God can take care of all you problems." It is true. All things are possible with God and I've seen Him solve some problems that there just didn't seem to be any solution possible. But if the only reason to turn to God is to get out of trouble, whatever the problem might be, it just isn't grounds for a permanent relationship between God and the recipient of God's graces. God can turn the biggest problem around until it is nothing and the person helped can be extremely grateful, but as time goes by that grateful memory fades and unless there is something else there, the old selfish nature of man will sooner or later resurface and things will be as bad as they were before. (Even Solomon in all his wisdom had a tendency to forget the grace of God after he grew old. It takes more than gratitude to have that relationship with God.)

There are other ways that are used, but there is only one way that can be permanent. That is the way of love. After all, God is love. Love is the most powerful emotion, the strongest bond that can be. It is only when we come to God in love and learn of Him that the bond will last. It's more than walking down the aisle and shaking hands with the preacher and saying we accept Christ as our Savior. It's more than going to an altar and shedding tears and saying the sinner's prayer. These are outward signs that need to be, but the real thing takes place in the heart when you realize the love that God has for you that caused Him to send His Son Jesus to die on the cross for your sins. When you realize the love for you that was required for Jesus to allow the soldiers to beat Him, to torture Him, to humiliate Him, you begin to love Him. It is not fear or personal gain that begins to bond you to your Savior, but love. As you learn more and more of what Jesus did for you, your love has to grow more and more. That love for your Savior can become so strong as to dominate your life. As a matter of fact, it is only that love that will be strong enough to let God use us as He wills. Any other service without love is just busy work.

It was love that moved Christians of old to be strong enough in the faith to die for it, to be tortured for it, to be crucified for it. Would your faith be strong enough for that, or would you look for different religion?

When you have truly accepted Jesus Christ as your Savior, with no reservations, no holding back in any way, then you become reconciled to God. Through prayer you can commune with God. Since He is alive and well, He can hear every prayer you offer-and because of the relationship between you and His Son Jesus, He will answer. It is an awesome thing to have God, the Creator of the universe, speak to you.

God can hear and accept your praise and worship of Him and the more you learn of God and His love for you, the more you have to praise and worship Him about.

It is too bad that so much of the time the churches program, that is, man's program, takes precedence over what God would have man to do. The church preaching and teaching what a man thinks should be preached or taught, or a board thinks should be preached or taught, with very little thought as to what God would have preached or taught. Some would not even know how to find out what God would want to have preached or taught. But that's man's way, isn't it?

Chapter Nine

The Monster of TV

It wouldn't be right to put all the blame on people types without giving some credit to our most time wasting, demoralizing, and stupid contraptions, our television sets. (Now since the set has no thinking power, maybe I should not call it stupid, but if I don't then it must be the person turning it on that's stupid.) Television could have been a very entertaining, educational, and worthwhile piece of history, unfortunately the crap that comes out of it outweighs the good it does. This treatise has to do with violence. Television depicts violence in every conceivable form and some forms that are inconceivable. When our children are barely able to walk, they are put in front of a television set. The television set is supposed to baby-sit, to be a mother, be a father, in other words, to take care of them. As long as the kid watches the set, he or she is occupied. The kid is quiet. The kid is not underfoot. Everyone is happy.

But of course the kid is only watching Bugs Bunny cartoons and such, so it is all very harmless. Yes? No! Today's cartoons have every form of violence imaginable in them and there have been a few invented that aren't a part of Mom and Dad's imagination. For lack of a better name you could call most of the cartoons 'adult cartoons'. These little kids see characters shot, and the victims just get up and start over. They see characters get their heads cut off, then the head is popped back on and the character gets up and fights some more. The kid gets the sense that this is the way real life is, you don't really get hurt, you just loose a few points.

Along with the large dose of violence there is the gutter language. Even the cartoons have all the cuss words, four letter words, and just plain crude language that you would find with the lowest sleaze. It really isn't any wonder that the four or five year old knows a lot more yucky language than their grandparents do.

As those three and four year olds get older they continue to watch television, just more adult type programs. But even as the kid passes from cartoon to adult cartoon, to just plain movies of what have you, the violence continues. They see hour after hour of assaults, battery, shootings, stabbings, etc. (Many of the movies you can just count the number of pretty girls at the beginning of the show and you'll know how many rapes, bashings, and murders there will be before the thing is over.) And if there isn't a good murder program on, there is the Nintendo, Sega, or old Atari games. The latest ones are very graphic in that you can slug your opponent and he or she will really go for a loop. (No gender discrimination in these games.) Or you can shoot your opponent and they'll look like they're really blown away. And for the real blood thirsty you can use knives or swords to cut your opponent long, deep, and repeatedly-blood spurting, heads rolling-and it isn't real. (O, heard the other day that the latest big seller video game uses crow bars as weapons to kill. Not violent enough just to shoot someone, they now want to crunch heads with iron bars.) The kid kills, but the individual killed comes back to fight again with the punch of a button. It gets to the point where the game is played or watched with no feelings at all about it, other than the score at the end of the game.

Back before television everyone played cowboys and Indians or cops and robbers and there was a lot of shooting and yelling and arguing, but it was never a mind soaking thing like the television programs or television games. Kids can reach the stage where they have no feelings about violence, after all haven't they seen so many times where there were no consequence for violent action?

The adult type movies that have so much violence build up impressions in the older kids' minds that are false, but very lasting. Impressions that are actually unconscious ones that may never surface, but are there anyway. I don't mean they put the thoughts or the plans in the mind for going out and shooting up the world, although this has happened, but a numb feeling toward violence can take place that says everything is going to be all right.

For instance they see a movie where all the bad guys have machine guns. (Which are illegal.) (It's amazing how a machine gun with a thirty round magazine can fire five hundred rounds in a few seconds. That's without reloading.) The kid may see during the shoot-out hundreds or bottles explode, windows shatter, cars fall apart and burn with an explosion, while the hero standing out in the open doesn't get a scratch. Not even a ricochet bullet hits him. He is immune. The kid empathizes with the hero. The kid is immune, or so he feels. Or take a simpler form of violence. Here the bad guys only use fists and ball bats. The hero is beaten, bashed, and discombobulated. Three minutes later he's on his feet and going strong, slapping a few bad guys around, taking his girl friend out for the evening, running in a marathon, whatever. Now it's been a long time since I was a Navy Hospital Corpsman, but I can remember sewing up, splinting, and bandaging numerous sailors that were worked over in a much less professional manner. I can't remember very many of them that felt like getting out of bed for a few days after such altercations. When I see, in a movie, someone kicked in the face, or hit with an iron pipe, and it has little or no effect on the victim, I go yuck, because in real life bones would have been broken. The victim would have spent days in the hospital. Not so in the movie. Ten minutes a Band-Aid and some merthiolate and the victim is back for a second round. No problem. When kids see enough of this, it becomes ingrained in their thinking. It's no problem to hit someone with a ball bat, or shoot them, in ten minutes they'll be up and about asking for more. And when the hero terminates the bad guys either by shooting them or breaking their necks, you never see the hero have a minute's remorse. He or she never gets depressed over killing someone. It just isn't the hero's style. He either goes to a bar or has a drink, or goes out to supper, or goes and jumps in bed with the pretty girl. All that killing is put aside and forgotten like yesterday's garbage. This is the picture that the kid gets. The kid doesn't realize that there is a price to pay in real life. (Most law enforcement agencies, even the small ones, have policies that mandate psychological counseling for an officer that has been involved in a shooting incident. The officer may not have killed the person he or she had the shoot-out with, but usually they are upset enough to need counseling. Some officers even need some counseling when they are involved with a particularly gory crime, though they may not have to fire a shot or get physical with a suspect. But this is the kind of real life stuff that you don't see in the violent movies, or the violent video games. It's not what the kid understands may take place. His or her mind only takes in what's on the tube, and the mind becomes numb to anything else. I'll take television off the hook a little by saying there are millions of kids that grow up on television without ever going off the deep end and perpetrating some ghastly deed of horror. I wonder if that's because of parents that have put some moral values in their heads at some early age.

For all the violence that television and the video games have their part in, I'm wondering what will happen when the virtual reality games really come into their own. That is when they are cheap enough for more people to own them. When the kid, or the adult can sit for hours and experience all kinds of violence, can really feel that they have been involved in violence, murder, rape, and got away with it, what will be the next step up the ladder of thrills? Now it shouldn't take a rocket scientist to figure that one out.

Some time ago there was a fuss about the game Dungeons and Dragons, and games like it. These games combined violence with the occult and other unappetizing things. Some people claimed that the games got their kids so mentally fouled up that it caused them to commit violent acts, sometimes against themselves. Then the furor died down. Don't hear anything about it anymore, but I see on the bookstore shelves dozens of games along with books on the game of Dungeons and Dragons. Guess they must have developed a vaccine for the problem.

A close kin to the television, one might call it a cousin to TV, would be some of today's music. (Some of it is on videos, some on disks, and some on audiotapes, but we'll lump it all into electronic gadgetry.) There's been much talk over the past twenty or so years about the effect of some types of music on the nation's young people. The effect has become much more pronounced with the advent of rap music. Pronounced to the tune of being blamed for a number of very violent acts of murder, suicide, and other acts of mayhem.

Many adults can listen for a few minutes to some of the modern music and say, "I can't understand a thing they are saying." (Or singing. No, yelling would be a better term.) But if one checked closely what some of the lyrics in the music proposes, you'd find that everything from drugs to sex, to killing people is advocated. This includes suicide. To listen to the message once might have little effect on a person, but to listen to the same message for hour after hour, day after day, often so loud that the base actually jars your body to the rhythm, can have an adverse effect. The message gets into the subconscious of the listener like hypnosis. It is a form of brain washing just as much as any brain washing that took place in any war. The only difference is that it takes place over a long period of time and without the physical torture to speed the process. (Then again to some of us listening to the stuff for a period of time would be physical as well as mental torture.)

We could put another cousin of the television in here that is going to promote violence in the future and that is the Internet. We'll forego that bit of excitement because it isn't a big factor in the violence scene yet. It is used to give instruction in bomb making and such, but its biggest problem right now is in the field of pornography. There are also plenty of hate groups that have their web page on the Internet and as time goes by they will have their part in the world of violence. There has been much talk about putting some restrictions on things on the Internet, but since users of the Internet can get hooked up to anyplace in the world it's going to be almost impossible to keep people from using it to get their bomb receipts, poison formulas, and other plans for violent behavior distributed.

Chapter Ten

Gun Control

Now let's get back to the irritation that brought all this on in the first place. Gun control. And with the topic of gun control I'll bring in some thoughts that may sound pretty wild to you at first, but if you look around, read the papers, watch the news, and above all, think, you may decide that these thoughts are not so far out in right field after all. It is interesting to note that when violence is spoken about, who speaks and about what they speak. There seems to be one group that cannot speak of violence in the street or in the home without speaking of gun control. They speak sadly of the children that die from guns, the crimes that guns commit, and how easy it would be to save thousands of lives by controlling or even banning guns. (The same people usually have no sad thoughts about killing a million unborn babies, since that is politically correct.) The way they speak of how guns do this crime or that crime, you would think that guns had wheels and could travel around on their own killing and maiming with no human controls.

Personally, it is pretty clear to me what little effect gun control would have on violence. It is already against the law to shoot people, like in the drive-by shootings and the fouled up drug deals. If it is against the law to kill people, what difference is it going to make to the criminal to add one more small crime to his list, that of having an illegal gun? The criminal would get a laugh out of that. (Of course with our present criminal justice system the criminal would probably spend more time in jail for having a gun than he would for killing half dozen people.) It only takes a minute to look at the murder capitol of the world, Washington DC and get an idea of what gun control will actually do. Our nation's capitol has very strict gun controls. They are practically banned. Only the police, the elite, and the elite's bodyguards have guns. Can they control the violence? Look at the statistics. No one wants to walk down our capitol's streets after dark, and some of them in the daytime. In 1976 Washington, DC passed those strict laws. By 1991, fifteen years of total handgun control later, the murder rate for our lovely capitol had gone up 300%. Three hundred percent is a pretty big increase. The rate of homicides in the whole United States rose only 12%. Twelve-percent increase is too much of an increase, but it isn't anything like three hundred. In the past three or four years the rate has declined rather than increased. Could there be a direct correlation between most states now having a concealed carry permit that is available to law abiding citizens and the decline in violent crimes in the United States? You won't hear anything about that in the liberal news media. But it should tell you something about gun control when in nearly every instance of the city or state going in for strict gun control measures, the murder rate has gone up. There must be a lesson to be learned there someplace. Now since gun control would have so little effect on crime and violence, it makes one wonder if there isn't a deeper hidden agenda that these avid gun control proponents have in the back of their minds. But before I delve into some liberal left wing minds, using the term minds loosely, let us meditate for a moment about what the effects of gun control might be.

Incidentally gun control today is not anything really new. It would be the same thing as what the elite ruling classes of Europe did in ages past. The elite felt that the masses of ordinary people weren't smart enough to be trusted with weapons. (This was even before the use of guns-back in the days of the sword and spear.) The ruling elite had found from experience that the ordinary citizen was much easier to rule if he had no weapons to use in his defense. Even during the Middle Ages the common man was restricted to the tools of his trade. The weapons were held by a group of elite nobles under the rule of a king. It made it a lot easier to tax the common man, or confiscate his lands, or make him a slave. If the common man had had weapons and knew how to use them, many of the reigns of terror brought on by tyrant kings would have come to an abrupt end. This was something our founding fathers had in the back of their minds, and spoke of on many occasions. They felt an unarmed populace was a populace open to tyranny. That's why they were so careful to put that second amendment onto the constitution. They wanted the common man, the United States citizens, to be armed. That way there would be no takeovers by some well meaning despot wanting to be king. (And we have had more than one well meaning despot, wanting to make things easier for us all by doing everything for us from the cradle to the grave, while he became the king in everything but name.)

Speaking of that second amendment that so many liberals would like to see removed from our constitution. Some would like to see a constitutional convention convened to remedy such faults of the constitution as the second amendment. What is not mentioned when they speak of such a convention is that there would be no limits on what could come up for a change. There are other parts of the constitution that some people don't like—so if one is dismantled, then it could start a real landslide of changes in our constitution. Our constitution has been the thing that's kept us free and going for this long. It wasn't a perfect document and those first ten amendments left out a few things that should have been understood from the beginning. (Women should have been voting a long time before an amendment gave them the right to vote. It should not have taken an amendment to get the job done. Just as blacks should have been free and voting a long time before they did.)

If the second amendment is weakened or eliminated, it will open up a can of worms that no one will be able to get closed—and there will be worms all over the place. I'm saying it would have an effect on a lot more than gun owners. Samuel Adams said, "Let the constitution never be construed to prevent the people of the United States, who are peaceful citizens, from keeping their own arms." And George Washington said, "A free people ought to be armed." George Washington had no hidden agenda for the United States. He did not have in the back of his mind rising to power and becoming a king, or some other name. He wanted our nation to be a free nation. The things he went through in fighting for this nation did not change his mind. He would have vetoed gun control bills. The people that wrote our constitution were not dummies. They had had experience with nations in Europe that had kings, dictators, tyrants, etc. They knew what they were talking about and believe you me, people have not changed much in the intervening years. There are still people in the world, even in the United States, that would like to be king. There are some even in Washington, DC. But it won't happen as long as our constitution is solid, and our guns are in our hands. Another thought along this line. Cuba, before Castro, had gun registration. No big deal. It should have curbed violence, cut down crime, and helped to produce a paradise. Castro came along and he had guns. He took over, and the first thing he did was to confiscate all the guns. Only Castro and his men had guns then. It was a pretty easy job, since they had a list of who owned guns and what kind of guns they owned. No problem to gather them up, even if it was necessary to break down a few doors. Life wasn't so bad at first under the new regime, Castro had saved the people, but as the years went by, the glamour or whatever of Castro's government wore off. More and more people began to realize they were no better off than slaves. Could they stand up for their rights? Not hardly! They could stand up all right, but they would be shot down. They had no way to defend themselves from their wonderful government. So what is left? Take any boat, tub, raft, or log and sail for the U.S. Thousands upon thousands have escaped to the U.S. How many thousands have tried to escape and wound up as fish food is anybody's guess, but many of the Cubans still feel it's worth the risk to get away from Cuba and its' left wing government.

Now let's think for a moment about what would happen if in a fit of total madness, guns were totally outlawed. (Which is the ultimate goal of all totalitarian governments, a disarmed public.) Let us just say the government passed a law that made it illegal to have any kind of a firearm, except for the police and the military. (This is what our government is trying for right now under the guise of banning just certain types of weapons, or taxing ammunition.) Now let us say that in a fit of law-abiding insanity all gun owners turned in their guns. Rifles, pistols, shotguns, assault weapons, the whole lot. Do you think for one minute, for one second, the criminals or the too chicken to be criminals but would be criminals would turn their guns in to the government? Not on your life. The criminals aren't that stupid. With the law-abiding citizens unarmed the criminals would have a picnic. Any home, any business, any woman or man walking alone would be an easy target. You say, "But the police!" Bull! The police can only be in so many places at one time. Even in a small town it takes several hours to make a patrol tour. That means the officer may be a mile or two away patrolling on the west side of town while you are being mugged on the east side of town. The police can only come to your rescue when they are called, unless by a lucky accident they happen to be passing by when the mugger grabs you. If you have been tied up by a gun toting criminal and your throat cut, how do you plan to call for the police? Besides that, all the police, who by now have been Federally trained and indoctrinated, are now busy burning down some church where they think a gun might be hidden, you'll have to wait your turn. But you continue to whine, "But it's against the law for those criminals to have guns." True. True. But it's also against the law for them to do a lot of other things too. For instance, wasn't it against the law for that bank robber to rob a bank, no matter whether he used a gun or a stick of dynamite? He still robbed it. Wasn't it against the law for that guy to rape that woman? It was against the law to rape whether he forced her with a gun, knife, or brute strength, but he did it anyway. The criminal doesn't let a little thing like, "it's against the law," stop him. He goes right on with his chosen profession.

Now who is stupid enough to believe that just because it's illegal to have a gun that's going to keep guns out of the hands of criminals? I can name a few that are that stupid. I see them on TV quite often. So then some left wing bureaucrat backs off a little and tries a different route to reach their ultimate goal of an unarmed and docile population.

"Let's not outlaw guns, let's just register them so that we can keep track of them and have a tool with which to fight crime. We can have all gun owners have a criminal check up to make sure no guns get in the hands of the wrong people." This is pure bull. (Or can you have pure bull?) The criminal can get any kind of a gun he wants without going through any kind of registration. There are tens of thousands of guns smuggled in to the U.S. every year. No registration. No bill of sale. No nothing. There are thousands of guns stolen each year. So what if the gun is registered to Joe Clean, when his gun is stolen it slips into the crevices of the underworld. Once in a while they show up again, but very few are ever recovered. I know of one burglary where over one hundred guns were stolen. (Mostly hand guns.) That's been some ten years ago and I know of only two of them that have been recovered. Since they were stolen from a gun shop all of them had their serial numbers recorded but that didn't seem to help much. And who is going to pay for that gun registration? Of course, the gun owner. For fifty cents worth of paperwork the government will charge fifteen dollars, to begin with, more later, making quite a profit. A profit not to fight crime with, but to track down those terrible civilians that may have forgotten Grandpa's old blunderbuss in the attic and are now criminals for having an unregistered gun.

And what about that criminal record check up to make sure the criminals can't get their hands on guns? What self respecting robber, burglar, rapist, what have you, is going to come in to the police station and ask for a criminal record check? If he is that stupid he should consider another line of work, like politics. No, that burglar is just going to break into a store and take the unregistered weapons he wants and laughing go on his way.

Besides the above, at the present time there are lots of criminals that don't have a criminal record. At least not one that would turn up on a routine check. I know several men running around that have no criminal record that you can find routinely, because the records of their crimes were never sent in to the record repository, then as new people came into the department the old records were shredded and tossed out to make room for other neater stuff. In some very small departments even arrest reports are sometimes mislaid.

And that criminal record check. It's going to cost money. Where the department making the check will be out maybe fifty cents, the government will want maybe fifty dollars. Some poor Joe with never even a parking ticket will have to fork up a wad of money just to prove he has no record. It would be just one more way for the government to make it hard if not impossible to own a gun, thus disarming the public, slowly but surely. And that record check doesn't even touch on those time bombs that have a perfectly clean record, but have a drinking problem, a drug problem, or a very volatile temper. That record check doesn't touch on someone that is mentally unstable. (It's already against the law for a mentally unstable person to buy a gun, but if that person swears on the form he or she fills out that they are mentally all right, the salesman isn't a psychiatrist, so how is he going to know he's dealing with a madman?) The people that pushed so hard to get the Brady Bill passed now brag about how many criminal types the law has kept from buying guns. That too is bull. If a person is turned down for any reason he or she simply has someone else go buy the gun they want. (I turned down one application, not because the guy had a criminal record, but because I knew he had been in the state mental hospital several times. He didn't put up any fuss about it, just had his wife put in an application for buying a gun the next week. There was no reason to turn her down. I'm sure the man has a gun now.)

And then there's the tax on guns. The conniving characters that are so hot for gun control will no doubt decide that there needs to be a tax on guns that will pay for all the crime fighting whether it's crime by gun or crime by deception. That tax may not be too high at first, but it will become so high that the common man won't be able to afford it and will have to turn in his guns to the government. (After all he won't be able to sell them, so the only solution to keeping food in the house will be to turn them over to the government to destroy so that the former gun owner can get out from under the tax burden.) Don't be fooled. There are many ways to make you give up your guns without outlawing them. Taxing them out of your hands would not be difficult under the right circumstances. Any way you slice it, what would soon be the case is there would be no guns in the hands of the common man. Only the police, the criminals, the military, and the elite would have guns.

Now we know what criminals are and why they need guns. We know what the military is and why they need guns. We know what the police are and why they need guns, at least right now we do. But what if as the years go by, first the Federal government under the left wing elite, paid for the hiring and training of most of the police? Police officers selected by left wing politicians and subjected to Federal training that indoctrinated them in left wing policies. (You can see some of how this works now if you've seen how some of the politically appointed big shot police grab for those Federal handouts.) Those police would be loyal to just the left wing elite. They could become the right arm of the elite you might say. It's even possible as the military gets smaller and smaller, and more computerized, that it might become a second arm, the left arm of the bureaucratic elite.

Now I wonder why these liberal hearted left wing politicians and their bleeding heart sympathizers could possibly want the population to be unarmed? There are cheaper and better ways to cut down the violence. Could there possibly be a reason, a hidden agenda in the backs of their minds?

Let's fantasize a little. The world situation is not looking too good right now. The national debt is so big that it will never be paid off. The politicians talk of cutting the deficit like it was some great thing. That's the biggest bucket of white wash that was ever dumped on the heads of American taxpayers. What they are saying when they talk of cutting the deficit is just trying not to go deeper into debt so fast. If you spend three hundred dollars a week and you make only two hundred dollars a week, and you owe a million dollars, most grade school students would be able to figure out that you'd never get out of debt. Not only do you have that tremendous debt, but you're going deeper in debt by a hundred dollars a week. You have a hundred-dollar a week deficit. So big deal if you cut that deficit by fifty dollars a week. You're still going into debt deeper and deeper.

Most junior high students could tell you what happens if you go deeper and deeper into debt until you can't pay your bills. Unfortunately our government leaders can't figure that one out. But as long as the lawmakers can spend enough money to buy enough votes to continue in office, they really don't care what will happen to the generations to come after them. That's called self serving or selfishness. Or is there a plan, or a hidden agenda? When some of these liberals figure that the jig is up or the time is right, what kind of solution might they come up with to stay in the saddle? It might be something like this. Print more money. It has happened time and time again all over the world. Germany before World War II printed so much money and inflation got so high that people took baskets of money when they went grocery shopping. The more money you print the higher inflation gets. Problem with that is as the price of bread goes up, people on fixed incomes stay at the same level and begin to starve. The result is always the same, savings wiped out, homes lost, lives ruined. Or it might be something like this. (Same song, different tune.) One morning you wake up and see on the morning news that, one, all money has been scrapped. New money has been printed and will be put into circulation. The government is going to start over nice and new. Clean and fresh. This would eliminate the national debt. The government wouldn't owe anything. It would also wipe out all individual savings, all retirement funds, and all pensions. Most of the elderly would have no income at all. Most of the middle class would be bankrupted. The very poor, depending on welfare would find their source of income shut down. While still choking over the morning news the second blow is landed. Taxes on those that still have a job will be doubled or tripled. After all the government will need all that extra money to pay for the doles, bread lines, and other perks to keep all those bankrupt people alive. The elderly too will have to be taken care of, as will the millions of unemployed. What you wind up with is a type of socialism that looks, smells, and tastes like communism. All the rules will even be made, naturally, by an elite class of very wealthy people. Now you say the people would never stand for such a rotten deal? Oh wouldn't they? Are you forgetting that the people, the population, the common man, is unarmed? The only people with weapons are the police. Police that are selected, trained, indoctrinated, and paid by the Federal government, and the military, selected, trained, indoctrinated, and paid by the Federal Government. Now just what can Mr. John Q. Public do? Not much. He can moan and groan, but there wouldn't be anything he could do, except to line up to get his monthly dole and when he gets sick, his socialized medicine. This is the kind of thing the framers of the constitution tried to make sure could not happen when they put that second amendment in the constitution. They could envision what could happen to an unarmed population.

Let's take this new government a step farther. What about all those elderly people? It takes a lot of resources to take care of them. Now if it is legal to kill unborn children, would the next step be to terminate the elderly, or the handicapped, or those that were no longer productive? They might not just take them out and shoot them, but if after age sixty-five, or sixty, or whatever, if access to medical services were denied, the elderly would be cut down drastically. They then might consider the same thing for the handicapped or even the nonproductive. America could go from a democratic government to a dictatorship by the elite with the stroke of a pen.

It would not be an overnight thing. They would have to work up to it, but one of the first and biggest steps would be to disarm the people. That's what England wanted to do to the colonies. Disarm them, then they would not have the means to fight back. England had ordered the colonists to turn in their guns on a certain day at a certain place. But the colonists did have arms and they were not thinking about a revolution against England when that first shot was fired, but once it was started, the

American colonists finished the job. There was a price to pay for our freedom though. Many good men died on both sides. Blood paid for all of those freedoms our founding fathers achieved.

That's why the fathers of our country, with much foresight, put that second amendment in the Bill of Rights. The right to bear arms. The writers of the constitution knew that had they been unarmed, they would not have had a chance. So they made it a part of our constitution to protect that right of free people to protect themselves from tyranny. England wasn't the first to practice disarming her subjects. Rome did it to the countries it conquered. Roman legions would conquer a people, disarm them, then scatter them, and then put them to work. Docile slaves.

Even before that we have the record of what was done to the nation of Israel in the Old Testament. In many instances when Israel was conquered, all weapons were confiscated, and destroyed. King David had a hard time finding a weapon to defend himself at one time. But it seemed a regular thing for some nation to conquer Israel, disarm the people they didn't kill, scatter them, and domesticate them. (Of course the Jews never became docile. At least most of them didn't. You could always find a few of the elite that would be willing to sell out to the enemy for money, power, or position.)

"Oh!," you say, "Our government would never do a thing like that. It wouldn't be the will of the people." Since when have most elected officials worried about the will of the people? Since only a few people bother to vote, and a lot that do vote don't have the foggiest idea of what the person they voted for really stands for, the politician knows that if he greases enough of the squeaky wheels and doesn't get caught shooting someone, he has it made. (Look at those in office today that have been caught using illegal drugs, stealing, racketeering, and so on, and are still in office and you might think you can even get away with murder and still be reelected. (Obviously you can have a felony convection for cocaine and still get elected to some offices, as per a neighboring state.) But never mind the elected officials. They seem to have little power in the government in the long run. Think about the bureaus that really run the government. Like the IRS. Elected officials sometimes get elected with the idea of going to Washington and cutting down on the bureaus, the huge numbers of paper shufflers, the red tape, only to find that everything is so engrained that they can't do anything.

Which reminds me. All this bull about assault weapons. It is nauseating the way the bleeding heart liberals make a big deal out of assault weapons. They either scream hysterically or they speak so softly and reasonably about getting the assault weapons off the street and stopping the violence. That's the biggest bunch of bull that has come along in years. How many of those drive by shootings the news media makes so much about were done with assault weapons? Practically none. How many of those drug dealers carry an M16, AR15, or an SKS? Not many. They just don't fit into the pocket very well. Neither are the rest of the banned assault weapons very concealable. (But on those TV shows you do see a lot of those assault weapons being used, and in the full automatic mode. Makes you wonder if the liberals can tell the difference between a movie and real life.)

Since not many people have an M16 or AR15, it's a lot easier to hit the owners of them than the owners of other types of guns, since the few can't make as much noise as the noise that would come from most households if all weapons were banned. But if you can get one type of weapon banned, the bureaucrats in such organizations as the ATF can twist the law around until it affects more and more of the weapons not originally named. Is it possible that some of the fat politicians pushing for the assault rifle ban have set there in their Washington penthouses, stuffing themselves and watching TV and have become so fat headed that they actually believe what they see on Miami Vice and a few other violent type programs? I can just picture some of them whimpering softly as some guy on TV shoots five or six people, picks up his date, and goes out for a steak dinner. Bull! Very few people can shoot even one person and not have serious psychological problems. (There are exceptions to that rule, as some of the drug people can do it without any feelings. Some of the foreigners that come in to the U.S. have no feelings about killing. Socio-paths have no feelings about killing. Clint Eastwood can shoot three or four, light his cigar and walk off into the sunset. But the ordinary man can't do that.)

On TV assault rifles are the in thing. I even saw one program where all the pretty girl warriors were armed with Steyr semiautomatic rifles firing as automatic rifles. Nice! (The rifles that is, well the girls too. But very, very expensive. The rifles that is. Not many can afford one, and the street criminal wouldn't consider one.) And the vicious violence. The politicians probably believe, since they've seen it on TV, that a 147 grain bullet will knock a 147 pound man across the room. That would be about like a man on a bicycle knocking a train off it's tracks. It violates the laws of physics. If you want to see a real increase in violence, violence to innocent people, violence to the elderly, to the weak, then take the guns away from the American people. For awhile it will be a terrible place to live. The criminal elements will have a real picnic. The usual law enforcement community would be unable to cope with the situation, so what would be called for? A national police force to protect us. We could call it the NPF. Russia called theirs the KGB. Germany called theirs the Gestapo. But when the NPF, the National Police Force comes in, abolishes civil rights, puts in martial law, things will calm down. With the establishment of this fine force there would really be no need for local police, except as assistants to the NPF. The government, the elite, could then run things by decree. (Note I didn't say rule things) There would be no need for congress or other governmental units, just a waste of money. They could be dissolved. Who would or could object? At least object and stay out of jail. At that point the United States would no longer be a democracy but a nation enslaved, ruled by an elite group of people caring only for themselves, but doing it for the masses. Once the army or the National Police Force has established martial law, then those in power can pass any kind of law they wish. (For the good of the people of course.) They can take your money, they can take your land, and if you have outlived your usefulness it shouldn't be but a step or two down the road and they can take your life. (After all, that would solve the social security problem wouldn't it? They might decide that at age 70 you were no longer a necessary item to have around. Who would stop them from such a plan? Not an unarmed population for sure.)

In the 1994 elections it would seem that the masses of the people had awakened and spoken. It would seem gun control was a dead issue. Oh contrare. The liberals behind the push for gun control are still there. They still use every chance they can get to plug for gun control. Disarming the American people is not a dead issue. It's there, not being pushed ahead so fast, but given an opportunity the left wing elite will push ahead.

And meantime the ATF will go about enforcing not the law of the land or the will of the people, but the agenda that the liberals have set up for them over the years. Truly the Alcohol, Tobacco, and Firearms division of the Federal government is a division out of control. It answers to no one. It can set up people as criminal, it can murder people, and it doesn't have to answer to anyone. It, like a number of other federal bureaus, has made it's own set of laws. Much like the IRS it has it's own agenda, it's own set of rules.

It was sickening to hear the liberals try to blame the April 1995 Oklahoma City bombing on the antigun control people. A terrible bombing with so many men, women and children killed, and the head of Handgun Control Inc. took the opportunity to blame it on those against gun control. As horrible as that bombing was, it didn't have anything to do with guns. Many of the liberals that yell so loud for gun control may not have in the back of their minds the ruling of America by an elite class. They however, have been so indoctrinated for so many years that they can only parrot, "get the guns out of the hands of the public." This isn't new. The liberal stuff started many years ago. It was taught to news people and commentators by liberal (sometimes-communist) college professors and now it's such a part of their heritage there is no reasoning with them. (I recall having to take a college course in philosophy several years ago. My major was Biology and the head of the Biology Dept. warned me that the professor teaching the Philosophy course was a left-winger. He didn't use the term left-winger. He called him a socialistic weirdo, so I was prepared, almost. The Philosophy professor ran down just about everything American in the semester I took the course. He did it in a joking manner, but starting with the American Legion he covered the spectrum of Americana. That was one course, and I had been warned. Think of some of those students that sit through class after class, year after year, of running things American down. They begin to accept that philosophy, then go out and espouses it.

It is going to be necessary to educate several generations to the truth in order to stave off what the elite liberal classes have in mind for us. Unfortunately, there isn't that much time. At the rate we're going, with the violence, drugs, breakdown of society, and the material problems that are prevalent in the world, we don't have a couple of generations of time to get the job done.

Another factor that of late has begun to enter into this yammering for gun control is the foreign influence that is showing up. The United Nations organization is working on gun control or disarmament on a global scale. There are resolutions pending that would disarm the population of the world, with the exception of an elite force of UN police. One very interesting point here is that it's Japan that is really pushing for global disarmament. If I remember correctly it was Japan that made a sneak attack on Pearl Harbor and plunged us in to World War II. It was Japan that bought up our scrap metal, made it into guns, then used it to kill thousands of our soldiers, sailors, and marines. If Japan had had better statisticians for their armed forces, they would have attacked the West Coast of the United States immediately after attacking Pearl Harbor, then the only defense we would have had would have been individuals with their personal weapons to defend the United States. Much of the U.S. could have been captured before the U.S. could have mobilized, if it ever could have gotten mobilized. Now Japan wants us to give up not our scrap iron, but our personal firearms. That's enough to make you wonder. You say Japan is such a nice civilized modern nation that they would never try that attacking the United States business again? Maybe so. But there are other nations in the would that are overcrowded and needing more space. There are other nations that have millions of hungry people that look at us and see plenty of food.

Since I've mentioned the United Nations, let's hit one more point. An arm of the United Nations has just done a study and released a report on the death penalty. They say we, the United States, are a cruel and barbarous nation that should give up the death penalty as a nation and use some other form of rehabilitation for our criminals. Now that strikes me as being a little strange, coming from an organization that has members that have allowed hundreds of thousands to starve. It has member nations that have tried genocide, ethnic cleansing, etc. It would seem the few murderers that we barbarically terminate would be a very small thing compared to the thousands, no millions that have been staved to death, hacked to death, and even shot in Africa or in a number of other civilized member nations of the esteemed United Nations. But never mind all that. I'm sure that the real reason for the whole thing is just trying to exert a little more influence over the United States. The United Nations would like to run the United States. (And especially to get its hands into the money tills of the United States.) Not surprising there are those in the United States wanting a one world government that would be very happy for the United Nations to be that government. That's how little some of our left wing citizens care for America.

Let's look at it this way. There was a murderer that tortured, raped, robbed, and did other acts of yuck. Some men with guns caught him. He was sentenced to life in prison. But while in prison a lot of the peoples taxes went to train him, to counsel him, and to rehabilitate him. Because he became such a nice guy, even got religion, it was decided that he could benefit society if he were paroled. He was paroled. Once he got out he became an advocate of getting rid of all guns. Now there was a large group of people that OOOOhd and Aaaahd over this reformed man, such a sweet thing. So kind and gentle. They just backed his philosophy one hundred percent. He couldn't possibly do anything bad. Now would you be a little suspicious of him? Or would you just say, "Yes, yes, take my guns. You're right. Take my guns and get rid of them." I think I might wonder what his agenda actually was. I think I'd keep my guns until I was sure his agenda was for the good of mankind. (That would probably be when he died of old age.)

Japan is really a nice nation to pattern one's own nation after. The citizens don't have any guns so you should feel safe. However, their police force can use their clubs freely without fear of lawsuits. The police can break down your front door and enter your home at any time of the day without a search warrant. Just suspicion is all that is necessary for them to enter and search, or arrest and question. Their questioning of arrestee is sometimes given emphasis by the use of their clubs to help the arrestee's memory. You may be in the slammer for a long time and never go to court. (And they want to teach us how to live a quiet peaceful life.) Personally as far a Japan is concerned, they may be very sincere, but I want to keep my guns until I'm sure they are, which will be a long time from now. Japan feels they were abused by having a couple of atomic bombs dropped on them. I don't feel they were abused at all. I don't feel we need to apologize to them at all for those bombs, after all, we didn't start the war. We didn't want the war. And during that war the Japanese did some murdering, torturing, raping, and other acts of yuck. If you are in a war and you get killed, I don't think it would make much difference whether you were blown up by an atomic bomb or a plain old high explosive bomb. Like the murdering rapist in the foregoing story, who was caught by the men with guns, if he got a broken nose and a few bruises during his capture, it was nothing compared to what he had done to get caught in the first place.

Back to the United Nations. There are people in the United States, even in government, that are so set on a one world government that they would do anything to achieve that goal. Some would go so far as to betray the Untied States to get the job done. Of course they would say it is for the betterment of mankind. If the citizens of the United States could be forced to give up their firearms it would allow the United Nations troops a free hand to come in and bring order in just about any little disturbance that might come along. The UN would make the laws and their police force would enforce them. You say, "But our troops would not allow that." Bull. Our troops, what few we would have would be under some foreign commander overseas someplace doing some kind of traffic control. The troops enforcing the law here would be from some third world country where life is very cheap and things like troops murdering, raping, and robbing are quite common.

Speaking of our troops and how few there are today. Have you noticed how many military bases have been closed over the last few years? And with each base closing that means fewer and fewer soldiers, marines, sailors, or airmen. Now it's true we don't need as many service personnel as we needed during the four wars we've had this century. We don't even need as many as we had for the cold war. But the liberal thinkers are thinking we need practically none. Just a few high tech technicians to run all the computerized high tech equipment. Two problems come to mind. One, all that fancy high tech equipment is not as fancy high tech as they would have you believe. (During the Gulf war they sang praises about those wonderful Patriot missiles that could knock a scud missile out of the sky in nothing flat, or a smart bomb that could unlock a bunker door, tip toe inside and POW! After the war, much after, it comes out that those jobs weren't as accurate or as good as the news reports had them.) Second, if our soldiers are spread all over the world, Central America, Bosnia, Germany, Japan, Korea, etc. etc., and something comes up, what happens then? What if our forces get so weak and spread out that some deprived country with a larger army hits us? Like Cuba? Or Korea? Or China? Maybe the United Nations, as our protector would send in Chinese troops to defend us, or Mexican troops even. Do you suppose they would leave quietly after the melee was over? I think not.

If things like the above should come to pass and we were an unarmed population, there would be nothing that we could do. If we stay an armed population, we could at least put up a fight against aggression. We might not be able to resist the modern weapons the UN could put in the field, but we could try. As Patrick Henry said, "Give me liberty or give me death." He felt liberty was worth fighting for and I think there are still plenty of Americans that feel the same way.

One last thought on gun control. This has been much on my mind since learning of China stealing our nuclear secrets.

It is pretty common knowledge that there are starving people in China. It is also common knowledge that China has a much larger armed forces than we have. Now they have our best technical knowledge. (Along with some of our most sophisticated electronic equipment, thanks to some money hungry traitors in the United States.) Suppose for a moment that China decided the fastest way to feed her hungry people was to take over the United States. If China shot a dozen nuclear warheads over here, using our guidance technology, and knocked out several of our defense centers, along with Washington, DC, total confusion would reign. (I'm sure China has mapped every one of our ever so secret defense centers, and has all the necessary data all neatly plotted just in case. With most of our defense forces overseas and the few over here incinerated, what would be China's next step? Land a million man army on the west coast and start to take over. About the only thing we could do is all that have guns could try to stop them. Oh yes, while China might start it, Cuba would very quickly enter in by hitting Florida. (China has been advising Cuba on some military matters for some time now.) The United States would be under attack from the east and the west. (I wonder what Mexico, our friendly drug supplying neighbor to the south would do? Would Mexico still think Texas should be a part of Mexico?)

Any way you slice it, the United States would be in trouble. You'd better hope that all the gun owners in the United States know how to shoot, and still have their guns to shoot or learn the Chinese or Spanish words for I surrender.

When first I heard of the Chinese stealing our secrets the first thing that came to mind was what they might use those secrets on-us. That's the US. United States. When I wrote what was on my mind about the possibility of an attack by China, I thought, "Oh my! People will really think I've gone off the deep end." Since then I've seen an number of articles by much wiser men than I, that say the same thing, as well as a couple of people on television commentaries that are concerned, so maybe I'm not so far out, I just hope that I am.

Finally, something to keep watching in the future, just for kicks. Australia had a tragedy in 1996 in the form of a mentally deranged character killing thirty-five people and wounding nineteen. It was terrible thing that put the nation into shock. Gun control advocates in Australia were very quick to jump onto this tragedy and use it for all it was worth. (Just as the gun control people in the United States try to do every time there is a tragedy.) The gun control advocates of Australia were successful in their efforts. Australia has for all practical purposes eliminated private ownership of guns, from air rifles to shotguns, rifles, and of course pistols.

Since taking away Australia's guns, homicides for the nation has gone up 3.2%. Armed robbery nationwide has increased by 44%. In the state of Victoria, firearms related homicides have gone up 300%. One of the sad things about this is that in the twenty-five years before gun control, violent crime involving firearms had been slowly but steadily decreasing year by year. Doesn't that tell you something about what would happen to a disarmed public?

Chapter Eleven

The Answer-God's Answer

So now you've heard most of the basic reasons for violence in the United States. Some of these reasons you no doubt agree with, and some, your pets, with which you violently disagree. So now you want the answer as to what will stop the violence. What will it take to make us a more gentle, peaceful, loving, and happy nation, and for that matter, what will it take to make the world a more gentle, peaceful, and loving world? (And we will have to consider the world as a whole with transportation and communication the way it is making the world smaller every day. Within the next few years the other side of the world is going to be right next door.) It will not be the Untied Nations that stops the violence, even though the United Nations would like to get a controlling hand into every facet of life all over the world. But the United Nations has demonstrated that they have as much power to stop violence as an ant. (Now Dad would have been more specific as to what kind of ant.)

It will not be the social workers that stop the violence. They are a contributing factor to the whole mess. They haven't figured out how to get their heads out of their rear ends yet, let alone how to solve such things as juvenile violence, and the violent problems with the adults have them totally snowed. It will not be new laws that stop the violence. We already have hundreds of laws that aren't being enforced now and those that are enforced are almost a joke when it comes to stopping violence. It won't be putting thousands of new police out on the streets. That may look good where the police are located, but if the criminals simply move to a different, less policed, location, that really isn't going to make the world a better place to live. With all the new police that have been paid for by the government, many many areas are still very much understaffed. (And when the Feds stop funding all those extra officers, who's going to pick up the tab to keep them on the street?)

It isn't going to be gun control that puts a stop to violence. Gun control would only make it easier on those that want to perpetrate violence, and there would be even more violence. (Besides there was violence long before guns were invented.)

So what is the answer? God is the answer! Not religion. Not the socialized church, but God. God through His Son, Jesus Christ, and by His Holy Spirit. The only way that the violent individual can become gentle or nonviolent is for God to change that individual. It has to be on an individual basis too. God isn't going to zap a whole nation at once. He works by His Holy Spirit, one individual at a time. (Once three thousand in one day, but for the most part, it's one at a time.) And the only way that God moves is through His Son, Jesus Christ.

Through Jesus Christ and by His Holy Spirit. Men and women, boys and girls, many people of all kinds, colors, shapes, and creeds have tried to make themselves into better, kinder, gentler, just nicer people. Very few succeed. Most that try to be better, less violent, whatever, succeed only as long as things in their lives are running smoothly. When adversity strikes, the old nature returns with a roar. Our selfish nature is just pretty hard to keep under control. You may have a nasty temper with a hair trigger that can set that temper off with just a touch of conflict. If you are such a person you've probably made New Year's resolutions, vows, and/or promises to keep that nasty temper under control. You've determined to become a new person. A kind, gentle and above all a patient type of person. And how many times have those resolutions or vows come to a blazing end when that temper flared like Fourth of July fireworks? Sometimes even at the slightest provocation. It is very difficult to change one's personality, about as easy as for a tiger to change his stripes to spots.

That doesn't mean that all fail to achieve that lovable nature by their own works, as some become very nice people, but there are not enough that achieve that goal of unselfishness to make a big difference in the population of the United States, let alone the whole world, as far as violence is concerned. The only sure way to really change from the self centered type of individual is by allowing God to make the changes necessary and the only way that God will do it is through His Son, Jesus Christ. (I know, some will say that that isn't a nice thing to say because it leaves out the Buddhist, the Hindus, and a lot of other real nice people. That's true, but I didn't make the rules, God did, and He has known what He was doing for an awful long time, and His way is a proven way.) When a person accepts what Jesus has to offer, salvation, that person surrenders his or her life to God. That person has heard that Jesus came to pay for their sins by being an acceptable sacrifice for their sins, dying on the cross as their substitute, then rising from the grave to be at the right hand of the Father, conquering death and living forevermore. When one hears this, believes in their heart that it was all done for them, then that person accepts Jesus Christ as their Savior and at the same time becomes a member of the family of God. It is not joining a church or an organization, it is accepting what Jesus Christ did for mankind when He died on the cross for the sins of the world. By accepting Jesus Christ as Savior, God accepts you as one of His children, and as a child of God you can receive the blessings of God.

Many of the blessings of God include changes in one's personality, like the change from a self centered person to a God centered person. These changes may come very quickly, or they may come step by step as one grows in the Lord.

God is love, according to the Holy Scriptures. (I John 4:8 He that loveth not, knoweth not God, for God is love. And I John 4:16 God is love, and he that dwelleth in love, dwelleth in God, and God in him.) These scriptures mean that if we are God centered, we are centered not on self, but on love. We are loved by God in such a way that we want to love Him in return in the same way. This love, as we become closer and closer to God, reaches the point where we want to worship God, worship Him in spirit and in truth. The more we worship Him, the more we love Him.

As we learn of the love that God has for all of mankind, we want to love mankind in the same way that God does. We begin to love those around us with the kind of love that God has, a deep concern for their well being. It is a love that envelopes not just those that are kinfolks, or those that can be of use to us, but all of mankind. It is very difficult to get violent with those that you love. This love for others may not come as an instantaneous thing. It can be instantaneous. It can be if the surrender to God is a total thing and without any part of us being held back. (Some would object to the thought of surrendering to anyone in any way. It's something that comes naturally and that we've been taught as well. But to surrender self to God who is so wonderfully awesome, yet kind, gentle, and loving, is not like surrendering to an enemy.)

Usually we surrender to God, but hold back some part of our selves that we want to keep under our control. Maybe we enjoy whatever it is that we don't want to give up to God. (Or maybe it's some habit that we just can't get along without.) In that case the process of total commitment to God is a long drawn out affair with a little being surrendered now a little next time, a little later-slow growth the process of becoming more unselfish and more like our Lord Jesus Christ.

This surrendering to God only partially is usually because the person that accepts Christ as their Savior doesn't know how to totally submit to God and no one is around to teach him or her what it's all about. I've known several over the years that surrendered to God, knew in their hearts that they were Children of God, but didn't have the foggiest idea of what to do next. The result in almost every instance was that the person gradually slipped away from God until they were not even sure of their own salvation, then there was a return to their old ways and habits. As long as one is not totally surrendered to God, there is the very dangerous possibility that a temptation, a trial, or a stressful situation will arise that causes the person to give up on God and look to some other avenue for help or whatever is needed.

Some of the cults have forms of total submission, but it is always to a man and it always results in total bondage of the individual to who ever they've become submitted. Take for example the Jim Jones cult. Over nine hundred people were so totally submitted to that man that they all died for him. (Lately there have been other examples of cults doing practically the same thing.)

Total submission to God is a form of being made free from all bondage that would keep you from communicating with God the Father through His Son, Jesus Christ.

Perhaps part of the reason that man can't understand how to become a part of the family of God is that many don't understand just how man himself, or herself, is made up. You see, man, and woman, consists of a three part being. Man consists of body, soul and spirit. Now it is pretty easy to see the body. The body has mass, some more than others and it occupies space, again, some more than others and it blocks the view. If we're talking about our bodies, our physical bodies, we know they are the things that are the housing for five senses. Five senses that receive sensations from the world around us, such as tastes, smells, sounds, physical feelings, and things we see.

There are a few people in this world that never get much past that physical body and the sensations it receives or produces. They want to see things that get their bodies all a-twitter. It might be things of great beauty such as mountain scenery, beautiful flowers, or it could be something mechanical, as cars, or naked bodies of the opposite sex. (Oops. In some cases the same sex.) Whatever! Just to see certain things seems to be all that's necessary to satisfy their lifestyles. Others want to hear things, such as music of various kinds and that seems to set their bodies all a-tingle. (Some of the extremely loud music can set any body to tingling, along with the windows to rattling and pictures falling off the walls.) Yes, even the sense of taste makes slaves of some. They live to taste those exotic dishes or some not so exotic but just tasty. And of course smell goes right along with the sense of taste The smell of that food, exotic or whatever, makes the old taste buds tingle and the mouth water, and the teeth get ready to go into action while the vocal cords say "Ummm."

Perhaps the sense of touch would be the most auspicious sense the physical body has, that being able to physically feel things. Things such as the wind and the rain, a car being driven by you, or the touch of someone of the opposite sex. (Oops! Again I keep forgetting about those gays and lesbians. I'm sure God won't forget.)

At any rate there are many people that only feel they are living when these five senses are being exercised or titillated. They live to see different and more exciting sights, to smell, to taste, to hear, and above all to feel physically things more and more exciting to their bodies. It is their bodies that they want to pleasure. This is why so many young people get off to a bad start. They know only what their bodies feel pleasure in from the time they are babies, so they try and try to give it more pleasure as they grow up. Stronger booze for a more potent drunk. A higher high by sniffing paint or other chemicals. Different drugs to effect the body in different ways. And that old standby sex. More sex in different ways, etc., to pleasure the body. That's the physical part of mankind.

One of the sayings of modern day life is, "If it feels good, do it." Lots of people go around in just that manner, trying to sense things that make them feel good or makes them tingle. It's one of the first things that babies become accustomed to and as they grow up, say into their teens, if they haven't found something deeper in life they may continue to search for those things that touch them physically. Drugs, alcohol, sex, all touch them physically and appeal to their senses. Some older people never grow up beyond this phase of life, but continue throughout life trying to find happiness by doing those things that titillate the body. Now the physical body and all that goes with it can be developed. Just as body builders can work and develop a body with many large and conspicuous muscles, the whole of the physical body can be developed. All it takes is exercise, proper exercise that is, plus the right diet and rest will develop those muscles. Just as feeding any of the five senses will develop what that sense is supposed to detect. Example: Someone that just eats to feed the stomach may not detect some of the subtle differences in the taste of the food they eat, while someone that has really developed a taste for food over the years can tell you what each dish has in it just by taste. Or a perfume sniffer can develop a sense of smell that tells him or her not only which perfume they are sniffing, but whether or not it has any kind of impurities and what the impurities actually are. Or the trained law enforcement officer can detect by sight many details at a crime scene that the ordinary arm chair type detective would miss. All this is a part of our physical bodies which may be developed to whatever degree we have the patience desire, and genetic where-with-all to carry out. (Admittedly there are some exceptions but usually failure to achieve the maximum for any of these is due to laziness.)

But there's more to the human than a body. The human animal has a soul. You may call it emotions, intellect, a mind, or whatever you wish, but we'll call it a soul here. It is the thinking, learning reasoning, and emotional part of man and woman. You can't detect it with any of the reasoning, emotional part of man and woman. You can't detect it with any of the five senses, but it can affect the body in strange and sometimes wonderful ways. (Well sometimes it goes overboard in the wrong direction and gets the other parts of the human in trouble.) Man is constantly thinking, planning, daydreaming, sometimes good things. He is constantly learning. The thinking and the learning can affect the emotions and the emotions can affect the body. Such things as love, hate, or fear can cause quite a stir in the mind and in our emotions, this in turn can cause a multitude of changes or effects in our bodies. (Physical changes that is, some very temporary, some more long lasting. Some good and some bad. But just as some people go overboard with the physical, doing only those things that cause the body to respond or give pleasure, some concentrate on the soulish things to the extent that everything else is put down.

In some extreme instances the intellect or mind is fed constantly to the exclusion of the physical side of mankind. Just as some things good and some things bad can go into the mouth and then become a part of the physical, some things good and some things bad can be put into the mind. (Usually through the eyes, but some things enter through the sense of hearing, or touch, etc.) There is a scripture that says, "Ever learning and never able to come to the knowledge of the truth." 2 Timothy 3:7. When the mouth takes in something that's bad or poison, it can go into the body and cause sickness or even death. The same thing can be said about the soul of man. When something bad goes into the soul, into the mind, it can cause a sickness of the mind and in some cases death. Still some feed and exercise the soul until the mental faculties become like the body builder's body. Some feed the mind to learn more, some feed the mind in order to exercise or stimulate the emotions, which in turn tingles the body. If the soul is built upon good things, that's good. If it is built and exercised on bad things, then that's not so good.

The part of man that God is deeply concerned about, is the spirit of man. Man's spirit is the part of him that Jesus spoke of when He said, "You must be born again." He wasn't speaking of a physical birth, or a renewing of the mind, but He spoke of the rebirth of man's spirit. There is no way that by himself man can cause his spirit to be 'born again'. The only way that his spirit can be reborn and begin to grow is for the Lord Jesus Christ to cause it to be reborn. When a person accepts Jesus Christ as their Savior, their spirit becomes alive. The third part of the animal called human becomes alive.

Now with the birth of that spirit one might think that they are finished, that they have reached the pinnacle of being. Not hardly. The spirit of man, just as the body and soul, needs to be exercised. Needs to be developed. Unfortunately many good people stop at the birthing and go not on. It is like a baby being born, then staying a babe for many years or even until they die. A babe that doesn't grow up can be subject to many dangers that the mature adult is not susceptible to. The spirit of man needs spiritual nourishment just as a baby does. It needs the Word of God in large helpings. The written word and the spoken word. Most newly born Christians have this hunger built in and spend much time studying God's

Holy Word and the spirit grows. You've seen them, I'm sure, that are so excited about their Savior when they first are reborn that they attend every church meeting they can get to and read the Word night and day. But such a diet is not balanced and the spirit can stop growing just as the body would stop growing on a diet short of vitamins. Prayer is another essential for the growth of the spirit. Prayer is communicating with God. I said, communicating with God. That's a two-way communication. Not just listing of things you want God to correct, even though some of them may be very worthy. The kind of communicating I'm talking about is communicating in such a manner that you and God become closer. (Can you imagine a boy courting a girl and all he ever communicated to her was a list of things he wanted or a list of gripes he wanted corrected? That relationship would probably not grow very much). You say communication has to be a two-way affair? When you pray you're the only one doing the talking and God never says anything? God is alive. He does speak to those that truly seek Him. He may communicate by directly answering a prayer, or He may speak to your spirit if that spirit is developed well enough to hear Him. He may speak through His Word or through someone else that is sensitive to His voice, but you can communicate with God. As you continue in prayer, your spirit grows. Another facet of spiritual growth is the praising and worshipping of God. (That's actually what God created man for in the first place, to worship Him.) The more you learn of God and His Son, Jesus Christ, the more worthy you realize they are of praise and worship. Now Jesus said, "God is a spirit and if you would worship Him you must worship Him in spirit and in truth." To really praise and worship God takes all three parts of man, the physical body which is the temple of the Holy Spirit, the soul, and the spirit of man.

The body is necessary to get into a place of worship or a position of worship, while the soul gets into an attitude of worship or into a mental place of worship. (The body might be kneeling or whatever is appropriate, while the mind is focused on a marital spat or an unpaid bill, or what's cooking for dinner and worship will not happen.) With the body and soul under control, the spirit of man, if allowed to freely reach out to God can get the real worshipping done. One can reach out and touch God. It is possible to spend all of ones life developing the body or doing those things that touch on the physical and leave out the soul and spirit. Or it's possible to develop the soul into a giant and leave out the body and spirit. It's even possible to develop the spirit and leave out the body and soul becoming too spiritual to be of any earthly use to God. God wants us to be fully balance, body, soul, and spirit, so that nothing will interfere with our communication with Him. It's easier to communicate, to praise, to fellowship, with God, when our bodies are functioning properly and in the way He designed them. And when our minds or souls are clean and uncluttered with the sludge of the world, then the spirit of man is free to soar to heavenly heights in the praise and worship of our Lord and God. The church, (and I speak of the organized church, not the body of Christ), has failed in so many ways to get the message of Jesus Christ across. It has failed to live the life of Christ. It is so heart breaking to talk to some big pastor of a church and hear from him how the things Jesus said are not for today. To hear how people and times have changed and we should not expect to hear from God today. And that God gave men minds to figure things out for themselves, so the Word of God is really not necessary. Or that god is attainable through any religion, Buddhist, Muslim, etc., just as long as you are sincere about your feelings. And of course if you can't believe that everyone can reach God, no matter what their religion, then you are a bigot. A religious fanatic. Not to mention, not nice.

And those that would make themselves gods-have no need of the God of Heaven and Earth. No need of Jesus Christ to suffer and die for their sins to reconcile them to God, after all, they are gods themselves. (Now the modern educators don't use the term God, but by teaching there is no need for any being or source of power outside of themselves, they teach that each is a god. As those educators, whether they be in public schools or in religious seminaries, begin to age, begin to approach that time that we all must face, death, I wonder if they might begin to worry a little about-is this all there is?)

But back to Jesus Christ and His power over violence. I've talked about many things that are the causes of violence in the world today. Let me just remind you of a few. Let's take alcohol. In most of the domestic violence cases one or both parties have been using alcohol. In many of the crimes committed like robbery, rape, battery, etc., alcohol plays a big part. A man or a woman wouldn't do many of the things they do if it were not for the alcohol releasing their inhibitions first. The drunk, the alcoholic, usually can't help himself in getting out of the rut of alcoholism. Most of the time they won't even admit that they have a problem with drinking because they have convinced themselves that they don't have a drinking problem. They have to realize they are alcoholics and want to get help before anything can be done about it. And don't fall for the bulloney about alcoholism is a disease. That is one of the mushy mouthed ideas that the social worker types have come up with that is nothing but an excuse for not being able to help the alcoholic. I remember one individual that I went after in Topeka and picked up at an alcohol treatment center. A judge had ordered him there after too many DUI's and other alcohol related problems. He had been at the place for thirty days. As we rode back home he told me how he was dried out and he was never going to get drunk again. He was cured. But then six weeks later I took him home again after he was bonded out of jail after being arrested for DUI. He didn't understand how it all had happened, but obviously he wasn't cured. He cried and told me he needed help. I told him about the only one that could actually help him, Jesus Christ. He wasn't quite ready for "that" route or cure. He was going to try it on his own again. I know that a year later he served more jail time for the alcohol problem, and not long after that he died. I wonder if he was ready for "that" route by that time?

Another individual I came into contact with was also an alcoholic. I met him at a Bible study I was conducting in the living room of a private home. As I was teaching someone came in the back door of the home and

I saw this man stagger through the kitchen and lean against the doorframe of the door between the kitchen and living room. He was so drunk he couldn't stand up without support. I hadn't met him before, so didn't know who he was, but he was the husband of the lady that had asked for the Bible study. It was his home. I kept right on teaching and he listened for awhile, then he turned, staggered back through the kitchen, out the back door and off to the beer joint. The next night he came to church accepted Jesus Christ as his Savior and not only received salvation, but received deliverance from alcohol at the same time. For years after that he was faithful to his Lord. He became a consistent church goer, ever witnessing as to God's blessings, and eager to do whatever he could for the church. Many times he said that after giving his life to the Lord, he never desired to have another drink. He too died, but he knew what lay ahead for him and he was ready. Alcohol, meth, crack, crank, coke, whatever, all are big contributors to violence. God, through His Son, Jesus Christ, can deliver a person from any of those drugs, and can do it with no withdrawals. He can do it in such a way that the addict will not even miss the stuff. There will not even be the desire to use it again. Here again is where total submission comes in. God can deliver one from any kind of addiction, but when a person is delivered but continues to associate with those that use the drugs, very often the temptation becomes so great on the young Christian that they slip and try old habits again. When some slip up, they get or are put under such condemnation that they refuse to try again and may wind up actually blaming God for their worse condition. Jesus said, "I have come into the world, not to condemn—." He came to save those that were lost. His love does not stop when one makes a slip. Fellowship with God may cease but God would have that fellowship restored through His Son, Jesus Christ.

Another factor to consider that has lead to the proliferation of violence is the destruction of family life. The divorce rate someone has said has reached six out of ten families now. (But that doesn't include those that break up after living with each other for years without the benefit of marriage. There are thousands and thousands that live together, produce children, then break up. They don't count as divorces, but the effect on their children is the same as if mother and dad got a divorce. And the breakup is often even more violent than a divorce.) We'll not consider that most of those breakups had alcohol or drugs involved, since I've been over that point, but I've seen many couples ready to break up-and breaking up over what is called incompatibility for lack of any good reason. Couples that just couldn't seem to get along together. Some too that just wanted a change of pasture-looking for greener grass. I've also seen many of those couples turn in desperation to God to try to save their marriages. Many a marriage that was on the verge of going down the tube has been put back together by God through Jesus Christ. Many that were battlegrounds have become peaceful and filled with harmony. God allows the individuals to look beyond their own selfish desires and reconciliation can then take place. Reconciliation first to God, then to each other. Reconciliation first to God through His Son, Jesus Christ. Jesus said, "I am the way." He is the way to the Father. The Way. The only Way to the Father.

It is true that there are some couples that try, but that can't make it. Usually one submits to God while the other will not. When this happens there usually is a split. Often when one accepts God's will and the other for selfish reasons will not, the person that won't accept God gets even harder to get along with, since in their heart they know they are wrong. They get harder to get along with until there's no getting along with them at all. They may even begin to find fault with the God that their spouse has found peace with.

When both are willing to turn to God for His answers, there is peace in the family. It isn't a preacher that does it, or a counselor, but God. The real, living, loving God that can bring reconciliation. It may not come instantaneously, although it does happen that way sometime, but usually as problems arise that in the past would have been terrible problems, God makes the couple strong enough to surmount the problem and go on in peace. Thus the family can be preserved and in the process the children are exposed to God and His works, and they are less likely to get fouled up when they become adults. Plus the children too may accept the same reconciliation to God through Jesus Christ as their parents did. It all leads to a better family life, better homes, and less violence all around.

There were several other reasons for violence that I listed through the chapters. It really doesn't make much difference what the cause of the violence is, God, through His Son, Jesus Christ, can cause peace to come about.

When God created man, and He did create man in spite of what the evolutionists preach, He put into man and woman that need to love and be loved by Him. Just as God loved His creation, He wanted His creation to love Him in turn. He also wanted His creation to worship Him, but He gave man free will. He could love and worship God if he desired to do so. Man's love for God had to be based on knowing God, His love for man, and what He had done for His creation. But man failed God way back there in the garden when he first disobeyed by putting his own desires ahead of God's. Down through the ages man has continued to make God's will second place to his own will. Yet God proved His love for us by wanting fellowship with us enough to send His Son, Jesus Christ, to die for our sins, so that we could be reconciled to Him. By dying on the cross, He paid the price for our selfish works, so that by simply accepting what Jesus did for us and surrendering our lives to Him, we can be restored to full fellowship with our God. We can come into the presence of the Living God, Our God, and love and worship Him, fulfilling that deep need we have for His love.

I know, some of you think there is no God. When you realize however, that there is a God, and that He is alive and that through Jesus Christ you can actually come into His presence you know that you are loved. The more you learn of God, His Son Jesus, and His Holy Spirit, the closer you get to Him. The more intimate the relationship becomes, the more you become like Jesus, until all of those things that lead to violence pass away. And this comes about, not by just joining a church or going down to the alter and weeping, getting prayed over, then going back out the door to do the same old things. It isn't going to get the job done if your marriage is on the rocks and you go down to an alter and cry and ask God to do something, then expect Him to make all the necessary changes around you, without any change being made in you. It isn't going to do much good if you are an alcoholic, to walk down the aisle and shake hands with the preacher, say a prayer, and walk out without making that complete commitment to the Lord Jesus Christ. The alcoholic may stick it out for a few days, or weeks, or even longer, then a stress or friends, or just a slip and it's booze city all over again.

It won't help a lot to confess the Lord Jesus Christ with the lips-but not let Him into your heart, if you're trying to conquer a temper, a habit, a financial problem, or most any problem that is ruining your life. That going down to an alter, or walking down the aisle, or whatever the church does that you try out, may be the first step necessary to get you on the right road, and the words of the preacher has you to repeat in prayer, like confessing your sins and asking the Lord to come into your heart are necessary, but if it all doesn't take place in your heart, in your spirit, it's all just so many words and there will be very little change in you or the situation that got you in such a bind that you finally gave in and went to church to seek help from God. True, probably most people start to church because they are up against a problem that they can't handle so they go to get help from God. Many even go all the way to the alter, not really seeking God for God's sake, but for what they can get from God. They go for their own sakes. Some after seeing what God can do, then go ahead and make a commitment to Him and become what He wants them to be. Unfortunately some drop out just as soon as their problem has been solved, or they drop out if God doesn't solve their problems in the way that they would like for them to be solved. God does want to help us with our problems. He wants to help because He loves us. He demonstrated how much He loves us when He sent His only begotten Son to pay for our sins by dying on the cross. That kind of love is the greatest love that can ever be. Jesus, His Son, loved us enough that He allowed Himself to be tortured and killed on the cross, to atone for our sins, to make it possible for us to be reconciled to God the Father. Now there is no greater love than that.

God knows your name. He knew your name before you were even born. He knows every sin you've ever committed, even if you were a rotten drunk, dopehead, adulterer, fornicator, thief, or even a murderer. And yet He loves you. For God so loved the world-that was you and me, a part of the world before accepting the offer of God's forgiveness through His Son, Jesus Christ.

When you believe in your heart that God did these things for you, that Jesus died for you and that He arose from the dead and sits at the Father's side, right now-then you not only have eternal life, but you become a brother to Jesus and a son of God the Father. Then you can have fellowship with God. What does it mean to have fellowship with God? It means a lot of things that modern church people have forgotten about, like the wonders and magnificence of God, the power and awesomeness of God. Can you imagine going into the presence of the Creator of the universe? The Being that created and put in place the billions of stars in the heavens? The power, the timelessness, the omniscience. To go into such an awesome presence would cause one to fear and tremble and He would deserve your fear and awe. Yet at the same time His love for you would be so warm and close that you would feel the need to worship Him. Your problems would become small in the presence of such power. Self would become less important, only God and His Son, Jesus the Lamb, would have a place in your life, and whatever the violent tendencies in your life might be, He would smooth out.

There is a chorus that goes, "Our God is an awesome God." Our God is truly an awesome God. He alone has the power to change a person from a self-centered, violent, uncaring, unnice, type to a peaceful gentle, and loving type. He alone has the power to stop the violence, God through His Son, Jesus, and by His Holy Spirit.

Conclusions

So now that you've read the answer to all the problems of violence, the question is, is there the possibility that the people of the world, or for now let's just say the people of the United States, will ever come to that conclusion, take the step of faith and stop the violence? Will the people as a whole turn to Jesus and become a loving, nonviolent population? A population that puts others ahead of self. A population of Christians that are formed in the mind of God according to His will? The answer has been here for two thousand years and man hasn't accepted it yet. As a matter of fact man has tried to destroy that answer for two thousand years. In the very beginning Rome tried every means available to destroy the new religion Christianity. Thousands of Christians were tortured, fed to the lions, crucified, and killed in every way the devious mind of the Romans could think of to put sheer terror into the hearts of mankind. Our civilized lifestyle cannot imagine what so many of those early Christians went through. But instead of stopping the religion it grew. They couldn't stamp it out, so they did the next best thing, or worst thing for Christianity. They made it the state religion. They not only legalized it but they said, "Everyone is going to be a Christian from now on." They had some revivals. Roman soldiers would march into a village, accompanied by a priest, march everyone down to the river, baptize everyone into the Christian religion, and then march out. Now in that village there might be thieves, murderers, idol worshipers of various kinds, witches, warlocks, and even some just plain people. All were marched down to the river and baptized in the name of the Father, Son, and Holy Ghost. When they came out of the water the only change in them was that they were wet.

(Well, some of them that didn't believe in taking baths were a little cleaner. Not much.) Even though a priest might accompany the soldiers, he probably wasn't a Christian, just a political appointee. He couldn't tell the people much about Christ, and when he went on to the next village with the soldiers, he was soon forgotten. The people wondered for a while, "What happened?" Then they went about their business as usual. No change. (In the beginning church, those Christians that believed strongly enough in the Lord Jesus Christ to die for Him, did many marvelous works. God did the miracles, healings, and other wonderful things through the Holy Spirit, because of the faith of those early Christians. Those Christians that became Christians because they were marched down to the river and baptized without any believing in the Lord Jesus Christ could do none of the miracles or other wonderful works that real Christians could do. Christian became no more than a name some added to their list of religions they already belonged to. That did more damage to Christianity than all the lions and crosses that Romans had used.) Those converts the Romans made that knew nothing of Christ, sort of remind me of those today that go to church, walk down the aisle, shake hands with the preacher and become members of that church, without ever meeting the founder of the Church, Jesus Christ. They actually join a club, rather than become Christians. They have to pay their dues and they can even work up to high positions in the club without ever making any change in their lives, or I should say, with out ever letting God make any changes in their lives. (Now there are some that take that walk down the aisle and meet with Jesus, submit their lives to Him and allow Him to make the changes in themselves that God wants made. They then do make a difference in their church and sometimes even in their world. Those are the exceptions however, not the rule.)

During the Middle Ages the Crusaders set about to make the world a Christian world. Ha. Some of the most barbaric activities of all time were carried out by the Crusaders under the banner of the cross. The Lord Jesus must have shed tears as He watched robbing, torture, murderer, rape, and general slaughter taking place in His name.

There are many other examples of how man has used religion to hide his sins and done damage to the name of the Lord, as though he were trying to destroy the followers, the following of Christ. But of all of these ways of causing people to lose faith in Christianity, of destroying the effects of Christianity, or turning people to cults and some of the demonic eastern religions, perhaps the modern ones have come the closest to getting the job done.

By simply turning inward to self man has shut God out. It hasn't been a fast process, but it has been going on for several generations now. It is so widespread that it is taught in our public schools, the colleges, and even many of the seminaries. Many churches have turned from God to teaching and preaching the godhood of man. Since it has been taught and swallowed for some time now, many of the news media are thoroughly indoctrinated with the philosophy and any time anything or anybody does something that might rock the boat, it's time to get the big guns out and attack the unbeliever. (The Promise Keepers meeting in Washington, D.C. in 1997 would be a classic example of this. Some million men go to Washington, D.C. for a day, espousing basically the things Jesus taught, the things that Paul and the other apostles taught, and most of the TV shows were ready for a Federal investigation of the leaders to discover their 'hidden' agenda.)

All that is necessary is to really come out for what Jesus stood for and you're in hot water. The Promise Keepers were against abortion and that put them in hot water with the feminists. They were against homosexuality and that put them in bad with the gay/lesbian civil rights crowd. They were for the husband being head of the household and that got them accused of wanting to make slaves out of women. Yet all they wanted to do was do what God wanted. It's all in the Bible. Of course if you don't believe the Bible, then there isn't much to argue about. (It's amazing to me how God has taken care of His Word through the centuries. You would think it would change with the times. It hasn't had to change. Since God knew from the beginning what the end would be, so His Word, His written Word will be just as applicable on the last day of the world as it is today, and as it was in the beginning.)

But as applicable as the Bible is, and as many times as it has been proven, there are still many good people that don't accept it fully. There are even good church going people that can't accept all of the Word of God. They take out what they can accept, the parts that don't bother them and that allows them to live the kind of life they have always lived, the parts that don't make them feel guilty or inadequate as Christians, then the rest of it they say is for a different time, a different type of people, but not us. Those parts that are troubling are not for today. For instance, Jesus said, "The works that I do, you will do and even greater works that these you will do." (John Chapter 14, verse 20.) Now when most of the high ranking church people of today find that they can't do even the smallest work of Jesus, let alone something like raise the dead, they have to have an excuse and that excuse is, "That kind of stuff is not for today. It was for the early church to get the church off on the good footing." Bulloney! The works stopped when people stopped believing. Works are still done by Christians that believe and have a faith as strong as the early Christians. But getting back to the modern attack on Christianity. There are now millions of people that have nothing to do with Christianity because they are into the Eastern religions. Religions where you look inside yourself and find the inner peace you seek. You meditate until you find the answers within yourself to the problems that perplex the people of this day and age. It's nothing more than looking to yourself for the answers to today's problems. It's a process that hasn't seemed to work so far in history, but it has a fresh new start now. When one looks within him or herself for the answers, as much of modern education teaches to do, it is nothing more than putting self on a throne. With self on the throne, God has no place to reign. You can't say that the eastern religions produce less violence, for if you watch the news at all you can see where those countries where the eastern religions reign have more violence than we have over here. Violence usually on a much larger scale.

Will the people of the world accept the love and peace that God has to offer through His Son, Jesus Christ? With all these TV evangelists and religious missionaries going to nearly every nation in the world, you would think that the world might turn and become what God wanted it to be in the beginning-but I think not. I believe that some of the most violent behavior, violence unthinkable, is to come yet.

As the world gets smaller due to better and faster transportation, and as the have nots of the world see what the haves do have, they are going to try to share the goodies. Their methods of sharing will not come under the heading of nice. I think of the little civil wars in Africa, in the Middle East, and even in South America, and I think of the news reports of some of the so-called soldiers looting the conquered cities. There was the mentioning of rape and torture in almost every instance. The leader of one uprising in Africa was not present for the looting, murder, rape and torture, he was off in another place, dressed in a nice business suit, speaking on TV and looking very civilized. Another leader comes to mind in a different part of the world, Pol Pot in Cambodia. He says in an interview that his conscience is clear, yet he is responsible for the deaths of up to two million people after a civil war over there. He looked very civilized in his business suit on TV a few weeks ago. Those thousands that were tortured before being killed would have been very impressed. As long as there are people in the world like the above, hungry for power, hungry for wealth, hungry for the material things, there is going to be the potential for violence. In the United States we've led a sheltered life, but there are plenty of violent types here, and more coming into the United States every day.

A lot of that violence in the future will be directed toward the real "born again" Christians by of all people, the established formalized so called Christians. The so-called Christians that are politically correct, correct at least with man, if not with God. When the non-Christian sees the persecution of the real Christians, it will be easy for him or her to take up the sword to do more violence to the Christians. When life gets cheap in the United States, and it is getting cheaper every day, but when it reaches the level of that of Africa, or India, or many other countries, violence will abound. You ain't seen nothing yet.

It's interesting that some of the big universities out in the east that were started as Christian schools have begun to substitute different life styles for Christian teaching. Homosexuality is one of the big deals in several of our big schools. And since if you say anything against homosexuality or lesbianism they'll haul you in to court, nothing is being done or even said about it. After all, to condemn it would come under the heading of bigotry. Homosexuals, lesbians, those that practice masochism, beastiality, etc., are teaching young people the basic tenants of their perversions and those young people will go out to gain converts. But don't teach any form of Christianity. That's a no no. It isn't even politically correct to mention God, Christ, or Christianity. It might upset one of the devil worshipers, then the ACLU would have something more to fuss about. When the number of homos, lesbians, libertarians, etc., grow large enough, like a simple majority, they are going to begin to put down those that would speak out against them. The Christian speaks out against them, the Christians are going to be the ones persecuted. First in the courts, then in material things, such as taxes, then persecuted physically. Am I pessimistic? Only realistic.

One other thing I've not really mentioned that is going to be a real pain for the real Christians (the born again Christians). That's the news media. If you watch closely the media, especially the television and yes even some newspapers, you'll see a definite leaning to the left. Now it isn't a thing of some commentators coming right out and saying they'd like to see all Christians shipped off to the moon, but it's like leaving the Christian side unspoken or unreported and bringing out the side or cause of the left wing, liberal, homosexual, lesbian, or what have you. By simply emphasizing the view that they are in favor of they can make a lot of people begin to think the same way that they do. And note the movies, television programs, etc.

Slowly they have begun to slip in the propaganda that promotes homosexuality, lesbianism, gun control, and almost anything that might have a bad influence on real Christianity. (Guns aren't a part of Christianity, but a lot of Christians do have guns.) Any program that is supposed to portray real Christianity is skewed in such a way as to make it a joke. Programs that really do promote true Christianity are labeled as "right wing", and put in the same class as Nazism or even worse.

Do I think that the world will accept what God has to offer and become a Utopia? A heaven on earth? I'm afraid not. Many will accept God's answer and their lives will be changed wonderfully and forever, both in this world and in the world to come. The violence may remain, life may get awfully hard, but in God's hands there will be peace. Now I'll not put any restraints on what God can do. He could take over and make the world a very peaceful place indeed. He is that powerful. But that isn't the way God does things. He set up the way to make the world a better place and so far man has not seen fit to accept that way. (Jesus said, "I am the way the truth, and the life.") Man still feels that he knows how to get the job done better.

There is a way that this world can become a better place, but so far I don't see mankind as a whole accepting that way. But the way, the Way, is open to you-the individual. And God has His arms outstretched, open and waiting, for you. He has the answer, for each of us.

About the Author

Jack Eden was born in Kinta, Oklahoma, August 28, 1930. He attended school there through high school, then entered Northeastern University, Tahlequah, Oklahoma for two years. He joined the U.S. Navy in 1950 during the Korean conflict and served four years. He returned to Northeastern University after service and received a Bachelor of Science in Education in 1955.

Mr. Eden began teaching science in high school at Garnett, Kansas in 1955 while working on his Master's degree. He received the Master's degree in 1958, and continued post graduate work at Emporia State University, Emporia, Kansas.

He taught in Garnett for twenty-three years, until 1979 when he became the director of Community Revival Center Christian Academy in Ottawa, Kansas.

In 1982 he got out of the teaching profession and went into law enforcement as the Undersheriff of Anderson County, Kansas. This position he held until 1988 when he joined the Garnett, Kansas police department. From 1990 until 1995 he was Chief of Police in that department. He retired in 1995.

www.ingramcontent.com/pod-product-compliance
Lightning Source LLC
Chambersburg PA
CBHW061254280526
45784CB00002B/770